"In a world that is filled with an expectation for immediate gratification, we have lost the valuable, character building qualities that are established in us only through the waiting process that creates patience, endurance, and maturity. *In The Waiting* is a much needed book that will help you embrace the process and receive the wonderful benefits of endurance. I love this book."

—Dr. Patricia King
Founder of Patricia King Ministries
patriciaking.com

"Most us of us don't like to wait. We live in a culture where almost everything can instantly be accessed on the screen of our phones. Most of us don't create margin to wait as we are over-scheduled and overwhelmed. Tymme does an incredible job of reminding us that some of our greatest spiritual growth comes in the waiting. I believe you'll find hope, freedom and peace as you apply the truths from these pages."

—Tommy "Urban D." Kyllonen
Author, Hip-Hop Artist
Lead Pastor of Crossover Church in Tampa, FL

"I highly recommend *In the Waiting*. This is a unique book that will coach you in how to "become." There are parts of life processing that hardly anyone teaches about, because only those who have experienced this kind of development can share from it. In our generation, there are not a lot of people willing to go through this maturing process. In fact, some of our maturing processes are in areas we try to forget about when we get out of them. Like a woman's memory of pushing in birth neurologically rehearses the memory of the baby in her arms more than the pain of birth itself.

Tymme shares like a father, helping you understand spiritual transition and how to embrace your growth so that you can actually see fulfillment in the promises of God. You will encounter a thousand people who articulate a sense of promise and purpose, but only a few who will pay the price to actually walk with God and grow into His dream for them. This book will help you do just that. It's hot, it's vibrant, and it's full of truth."

—Shawn Bolz
Host of Exploring the Prophetic Podcast
Author of Translating God, Modern Prophets, and God Secret's
bolzministries.com

"Tymme is my good friend who will help you navigate the liminal space in your life in a way that lifts your head higher than the circumstance. This book is a must read for those looking to honor this critical process in our lives by helping us embrace God in spite of an utter lack of certainty."

—Shane Willard
shanewillardministries.org

""*In the waiting, I'm becoming.*" As soon as I read these words from my friend Tymme they seemed to leap off the page at me. Most of us, perhaps I could say all of us, struggle with patience. We want things right now. We don't want to have to wait. We really struggle when God doesn't do what we feel He should do in the time frame that we feel it should be happening. This is why I believe *In The Waiting* is such an important and timely book. Tymme is not just sharing theory but principles that he has lived out in his every day life. In these pages he gives practical teaching on what to hold onto and how to posture yourself when you are 'in the waiting.' Enjoy! Get ready to learn and grow! Expect to hear from God as you read this insightful work."

—Brendan Witton
Lead Pastor of Toronto City Church

"*In the Waiting* is a book that I have been waiting for! Pastor Tymme has mastered the skill of making complex concepts understandable and easy to digest and implement. During these transition times in our lives, it is critical to know how to approach them with wisdom and get the most out of them. This book opened my eyes to the beauty and potential growth of the waiting period. He empowers you to dive into it full force and not merely be a bystander watching time go by. This is a must read for anyone who desires to take their faith, and life, to the next level."

—Genein M. Letford
Author and Founder of Alumni360
2015 Charter Teacher of the Year
geneinletford.com

IN THE WAITING

MOVING FROM PROCESS TO PROMISE

TYMME REITZ

WESTBOW
PRESS®
A DIVISION OF THOMAS NELSON
& ZONDERVAN

Copyright © 2018 Tymme Reitz.

All rights reserved. No part of this book may be used or reproduced by any means, graphic, electronic, or mechanical, including photocopying, recording, taping or by any information storage retrieval system without the written permission of the author except in the case of brief quotations embodied in critical articles and reviews.

Scripture quotations taken from the Amplified® Bible (AMP), Copyright © 2015 by The Lockman Foundation Used by permission.

Scripture quotations taken from the New American Standard Bible® (NASB), Copyright © 1960, 1962, 1963, 1968, 1971, 1972, 1973, 1975, 1977, 1995 by The Lockman Foundation Used by permission.

Scripture taken from the New King James Version®. Copyright © 1982 by Thomas Nelson. Used by permission. All rights reserved.

Scripture quotations marked (NLT) are taken from the Holy Bible, New Living Translation, copyright ©1996, 2004, 2015 by Tyndale House Foundation. Used by permission of Tyndale House Publishers, Inc., Carol Stream, Illinois 60188. All rights reserved.

Scripture quotations marked TPT are taken from The Passion Translation TM, copyright © 2012, 2013, 2014, 2015. Used by permission of 5 Fold Media, LLC, Syracuse, NY 13039, United States of America. All rights reserved. Unless otherwise indicated.

WestBow Press books may be ordered through booksellers or by contacting:

WestBow Press
A Division of Thomas Nelson & Zondervan
1663 Liberty Drive
Bloomington, IN 47403
www.westbowpress.com
1 (866) 928-1240

Because of the dynamic nature of the Internet, any web addresses or links contained in this book may have changed since publication and may no longer be valid. The views expressed in this work are solely those of the author and do not necessarily reflect the views of the publisher, and the publisher hereby disclaims any responsibility for them.

Any people depicted in stock imagery provided by Getty Images are models, and such images are being used for illustrative purposes only.
Certain stock imagery © Getty Images.

ISBN: 978-1-9736-4369-2 (sc)
ISBN: 978-1-9736-4370-8 (hc)
ISBN: 978-1-9736-4368-5 (e)

Library of Congress Control Number: 2018912782

Print information available on the last page.

WestBow Press rev. date: 10/25/2018

CONTENTS

Dedication ix
Acknowledgements xi
Foreword *By: Faytene Grasseschi* xiii

1. I'm Becoming 1
2. Worth the Wait 12
3. Save Me from Boredom 23
4. Weary in the Waiting 33
5. Face Forward 45
6. The Making of a Masterpiece 55
7. A Storm-Proof Foundation 66
8. Times of Testing 80
9. Finding Freedom 94
10. Only God Can 109
11. Faith for the Promises 123

Endnotes 145
About the Author 147

DEDICATION

I dedicate this book, with deep gratitude, to my wife of 20 years, Aury. I would not want to experience the seasons of waiting with anyone else but you. Everything about you is beautiful and inspiring, from the love you have for Jesus, your zeal for life, your heart for people, and your out-of-the-box thinking and creativity. You are unique and wonderful and I love you dearly.

—Tymme

ACKNOWLEDGEMENTS

I especially want to thank my lead editor, Maral Hinson, for the excellent work you have brought to this project. You have been an inspiration to me during this process. Much thanks goes to Genein Letford, for your support and editing input. I look forward to your many books that will lead people to financial freedom and greatness. I also want to thank my assistant, Enjoli Duvall, for doing life with Aury and I and serving us well.

FOREWORD

In The Waiting is a tremendous read. Every believer needs this message, because every one of us will experience a season where we need to exercise the spiritual discipline of waiting as we lay hold of God's promises for our lives.

These seasons are not just about waiting for the sake of it. In my life I have found the seasons of waiting are essential times of preparation. Times when my motives were tested and purified, when my character was developed, when the authenticity of the call was strengthened, when my relational roots with the Lord went deeper, and when I learned how to pray my breakthrough in. Waiting for God's perfect timing challenges our flesh, but it is pivotal to our long-term success.

Recently my husband pointed out to me that one of my spiritual parents learned the value of waiting close up. This man was 47 years old when he began the ministry that he leads today. He recently said these words, "Let God give you the stage before you take it." It would not be a stretch to say that since stepping into national ministry in his late 40's he has emerged as a very influential Christian leader who is impacting the globe. Should the Lord tarry, his name will undoubtedly be recorded in the history books from our time. Yet, he, like so many heroes of the faith, had to be patient and thank the Lord for His restraint. He understood the importance of the waiting.

This book is full of wisdom and insight for the process called *waiting*. Tymme eloquently lays out truths from the heart of God in a way that a love for the process can be birthed in us. Thank you Tymme for empowering us and presenting strategies for reigning in the waiting. I am thrilled for this timely message to be shared with the world.

Blessings,
Faytene Grasseschi
Faytene TV / V-Kol Media / TheCRY / MY Canada

1
I'm Becoming

Waiting is a big problem. In our Western culture alone, "quick and convenient" is our addiction. We're much faster and way more evolved, technologically speaking. Just about every daily task you and I take on, someone has created a suitable solution to speed things up. The modern world is built to get you what you want faster and without breaking a sweat—yet ironically, we've become less patient.

At this very moment, I'd say we could easily presume that innovative companies are competing to improve a digital item or household brand to accomplish its purpose quicker. Who can blame them, when consumers are willing to dish out more money if the two-minute model can comply in one-minute?

Do not get me wrong; I am a fan of high-tech toys. I'm sure I possess some of the same gadgets that the average person uses to function throughout the day. The point here is to recognize that there is a menacing mentality deeply rooted in the traits of humanity that completely affects our spiritual advancement, and that is this: we do not do waiting very well.

You probably won't find patience towering at the top spot of virtues we diligently pursue. We do not like to wait, we do not want to wait, and even the sound of someone telling us to "wait just a moment" can disturb us. To a Western mind, patience can feel more like a punishment than a prize. Patience is only perceived as a way of learning how to cope with setbacks as we drag ourselves through difficult or delayed times.

In the book of James, he presents a belief countering the cultural status quo. His letter opens with a punch by telling believers they should be thrilled—better yet, joyful—when they experience the typical grueling, lengthy trial, because there is a bright reward in the testing of their faith. Yes, my friend—you will gain the reward of patience! That's right! The pay-off is enduring patience. This might not sound much like a win, especially if our relationship with the idea of waiting is traditionally sour; but it is actually one of the greatest outcomes we could ever hope for.

In the following verse, to reinforce his opening statement, James indicates what we should expect once patience and endurance begin to take form.

> "And then as your endurance grows even stronger it will release perfection into every part of your being until there is nothing missing and nothing lacking."
>
> (James 1:4 TPT)

Patience is not just a discipline or a method of restraint to keep us less agitated when things do not progress quickly enough. Patience is not the ability to "hang in there," or "keep your chin up," so that we persevere without causing too much of an annoyance to others around us. James reveals a greater purpose—IN THE WAITING, I'M BECOMING.

In that space of time, God is there perfecting every part of my being. Training, pruning, plowing, shaping, testing, and growing—until, as the scripture said, "there is nothing missing and nothing lacking" (James 1:4 TPT). To experience the freedom of living the full expression of what God intended for me to be, seems to always be constructed in the waiting. No wonder James invites us to express joy when we are facing a time in life where faith and patience are required. He knows that we are heading in the direction of destiny.

Make or Break

Waiting will always be a part of the faith walk. Nobody gets a way out, especially if we plan on following Jesus and finishing the glorious race assigned to our life. Perhaps you are in that position at this moment. You might be waiting for the Lord to lift a burden weighing on you; or maybe you're on a quest to build something pertaining to your calling and there are obstacles in the way. Perhaps you have been waiting for a certain revelation to propel a promise, or a financial breakthrough to lift a debt or fund a vision. Whatever type of advancement you are believing for scripturally or prophetically, in many cases, there is a process before the promise—and some will be longer than others.

So that you do not misunderstand my heart, I am a Christian who burns with faith for the here and now miracle. I live with a conviction that the power of God can arrive at the exact time a prayer is spoken or when a decree is released. I did not write this book to ignore that absolute possibility. Rather, I wrote this book to deal head-on with the topic of waiting, solely because that is the realm where many of God's elect either rise to new heights in the spirit or fall in a deep place of despair. It is a zone that literally makes or breaks us, proves our loyalty, and reveals the few kinks we still need to work out in our lives.

Either way, we will all experience the waiting. We will all have a chance for God's strategic, clay-shaping hands to form, fashion, and develop everything we were designed to be. We all know that an infant cannot possibly crossover to adulthood in a short period of time. They must develop through the natural stages of growth to blossom in age and stature. Similarly, we also require a pace that shifts us from one level to another.

Glory to Glory

In the fifth chapter of Hebrews, the author begins to reveal profound mysteries of the priestly position Jesus carried and how it is directly connected to Melchizedek from the days of Abraham. Oddly enough, in mid-thought on this subject, the writer decides to pause—and instead of taking this enlightenment further with his audience, he states:

> "We have much to say about this topic although it is difficult to explain, because you have become too dull and sluggish to understand."
> (Hebrews 5:11 TPT)

Sluggish was a phrase used to explain the mental condition of someone who would resist what it takes to gain progress. Somehow, something hindered the momentum of this group, resulting in a "spiritually-dull" state of mind, preventing any sort of progress. The next verse persists that they should all be much further along, since they have been believers for quite some time.

> "For you should already be professors instructing others by now; but instead, you need to be taught from the beginning the basics of God's prophetic oracles!"
> (Hebrews 5:12 TPT)

The expectation and nature of discipleship is movement. To constantly grow onward and upward, not just in age, but also in depth and intimacy, wisdom and revelation, strength and power; to always be advancing from one level of maturity in Christ to another.

> "...We are being transfigured into his very image as we move from one brighter level of glory to another..."
> (2 Corinthians 3:18 TPT)

> "...continue to grow and increase in God's grace and intimacy with our Lord and Savior, Jesus Christ."
> (2 Peter 3:18 TPT)

I find such pleasure in knowing that the Jesus journey is without limitations. We all have been given the potential to go further and further, soar higher and higher, with endless levels of glory waiting to be discovered. Considering that there is always more for each and every one of us, why do so many Christian lives fall flat, ending up stuck and stagnant? I believe one of the causes for losing momentum can be a lack of faith. For me to thrive, I must be comfortable with not always knowing or understanding everything. I need the kind of faith that excludes sight (not that there is any other kind).

Faith Not Sight

Consider the common seed of a fruit plant and how it can move from one level of "glory" to another. It begins as a tiny hard shell, that looks nothing like its final promised product. Yet, we surely expect and trust the seed to gradually develop, mutate through several different required stages, and to become what it was genetically programmed to be.

We have easily placed our faith in a cycle that causes a nothing of a seed to become a full-size harvest. Without needing to know the exact components wired within the seed that causes it to dramatically transform, we just believe it does. Is faith that simple? Could the faith we have in the laws of nature apply to the principles of faith in the spiritual life? Isn't it just believing without seeing? Doesn't that sound familiar? Let's map this out a little more with this passage.

> "Jesus also told them this parable: "God's kingdom realm is like someone spreading seed on the ground. He goes to bed and gets up, day after day, and the seed sprouts and grows tall, though HE KNOWS NOT HOW. All by itself it sprouts, and the soil produces a crop; first the green stem, then the head on the stalk, and then the fully developed grain in the head."
> (Mark 4:26-28 TPT, emphasis added)

The farmer *"knows not how"* the seed sprouts and grows, and that is perfectly fine because he does not need to know. That is not his job. Even if a farmer can recite specific verbiage that scientifically breaks down the agricultural world, that would not make a difference in his task. His main job is less about knowing how the seed sprouts and grows and more about providing the proper elements for it to sprout and grow. The farmers job is to give it enough sunlight, the right amount of water, and soil that sustains and nurtures its potential.

When it is necessary to wait on the Lord for something to

arise from seed-form to harvest, our main job and focus is not to always know the how and why, or the ins and outs—but to provide the right elements for the growth. When confusion and chaos are raging, and nothing seems to logically make sense, our only hope for survival should be to feed ourselves what is needed to keep everything alive, breathing and moving forward. The saying, "You are what you eat," is very true, because the seed "becomes" by what it is fed. And for us, spiritually speaking, we become what we consume.

What's on Your Plate?

You do not need to have all the answers (and trust me you won't) when you're traveling through any transition. Step away from the fixation of needing to be in control because you certainly will not win that match with God. Understanding everything is overrated and will not determine your success in "becoming." Again, focus on what you "eat," the elements you provide daily for your soul, and that will be the key to your up rise. Interestingly enough, Jesus also used "food" to keep Him aligned with His mission. He said, "My food is to be doing the will of him who sent me and bring it to completion" (John 4:34 TPT).

Jesus had enemies and lots of them—yet He always rose above them, triumphantly outlasting and outmaneuvering every conspiracy aimed to take Him out. How did our Champion do it? He ate "food." Feasting on every word that proceeded from the mouth of God (see Matthew 4:4 NASB), rather than the barrage of negative voices that seeped through the crowd. He spit them out, giving no room for anything that was not from the heart of His Father. As long as He controlled what He received and internally digested, no one had a chance of changing His direction or affecting His focus.

Think about the reactions of Jesus on the day of His execution. What came out of Him personified what was in Him. Never once did Jesus show any sign of aggression towards those assigned to torture Him, nor did He lash back at any of those who mocked and sneered at Him. Some have assumed Jesus was able to resist the temptation of "letting them have it," by mastering the art of self-control. That's not true. The real reason why He could not adhere to the thought of retaliation, or foster any negative emotion towards His attackers, was because these things emphatically did not exist in the heart of Jesus. He could not manifest anything but what He had consumed on His earthly journey to the finished work of the cross. Everything from the extensive love and compassion, the pleading to the Father to forgive His enemies, to the invitation of paradise for a convicted criminal who hung beside Him, was all a clear picture of what Jesus had become and what He had allowed to feed His heart and His mind.

He Wants You Free

To be able to exude a love that transcends any love we've ever known, on just about the worst day possible, is something that magnifies the freedom Jesus experienced in His life. When you can love when others hate, give when others are taking, forgive when others refuse to, you are immersed in freedom.

God paid a price for you to have the freedom Jesus modeled. In the waiting is when this freedom begins to find its ascension. In the waiting is where God unravels what's in us, what's anchored in our soul that triggers repeated behavior, what's holding us back, and what's keeping us down and bound. The waiting is a time to learn and unlearn, to renew and remove, to pull down, uproot, and to extract any rubbish in our life that can plague our progress.

IN THE WAITING

Not long ago, I had been nudging at God to establish the next leap for our ministry. He spoke to me, but not as I expected. The Lord told me, "In this coming season, you will need to experience offense, betrayal, criticism, and disappointment in order to experience the next level I have for you." Not the most inspiring thing He's ever said to me, but I knew He was up to something that would eventually give more than it took from me.

Before I share how this became an advantage to me, let's take a look at a couple of scriptures.

> "...even though lately you've had to put up with the grief of many trials. But these only reveal the sterling core of your faith, which is far more valuable than gold that perishes, for even gold is refined by fire..."
> (1 Peter 1:6-7 TPT)

> "...Even in times of trouble we have a joyful confidence, knowing that our pressures will develop in us patient endurance. And patient endurance will refine our character, and proven character leads us back to hope."
> (Romans 5:3-4 TPT)

Earlier we had James exclaiming that we should all rejoice when we face difficulties because it will strengthen our faith and our patience. Now we have another set of apostles, Peter and Paul, who also had a lot to say about trials working *for* us rather than against us. These apostles knew firsthand how "fire" refines the believer, and pressures develop these core attributes: patience, character, and hope.

If I must personally tangle through the ordeal of a trial, I definitely want everything I can gain from it. Some might be satisfied just to be done with it, walk away, and leave empty handed. I personally want every bit of wisdom and insight, every morsel of faith and power, and every level of maturity and strength that is up for grabs.

So, when God informed me that offense, betrayal, criticism, and disappointment were things I would soon encounter, I knew He was preparing me for something I needed. Although negative in nature, these experiences set in motion a freedom that I would not have unlocked on my own. Every incident brought to the surface deeply-rooted scars of rejection and abandonment that had become massive strongholds in my life; strongholds I did not know existed nor was I aware how severely it was impacting my ministry and my marriage in unhealthy ways. These strongholds needed to be dealt with. I could no longer carry them, as they would not allow me to go further into the destiny God was willing and wanting to take me.

Protecting His Kids

There are areas in our life that need to be taken away before God can add to us, lest the blessings harm us more than help us. Think about two belief systems trying to co-exist. That would not be possible, as something would have to go for something else to stay. Like impurities must be removed to give us drinkable water, in order for you to become, there are things you will need to let go of and remove.

So do not be dismayed when trouble is ahead. God is in the waiting, filling in the missing parts, and opening opportunities for you to experience new levels of freedom. Be patient and trust that He is a good Father, a Father who chooses to safeguard our lives by not letting us enter into a promise prematurely or underdeveloped.

A good military general will not send a soldier on the frontlines of battle without the proper training. A good parent will not let their child behind the wheel of a vehicle if they lack the skill to drive. In the same way, our faithful Father protects by always building YOU first before He builds your "ministry."

I would say the propensity of our impatience is commonly derived from wanting to be somewhere that we are currently not in our life. Where in contrast, God is much more interested and invested in you *becoming* something than for you getting somewhere—and in the waiting, that is when you are becoming.

> "I pray with great faith for you, because I'm fully convinced that the One who began this glorious work in you will faithfully continue the process of maturing you and will put his finishing touches to it until the unveiling of our Lord Jesus Christ!"
> (Philippians 1:6 TPT)

2
Worth the Wait

Did you know there are researchers assigned to study the psychology of waiting in line? It's true. Researchers have been given the task to find waiting solutions that satisfy the tolerance of the average consumer, and it has paid off big-time for those who practice what they had predicted.

It is said that billions of dollars have been gained and billions of dollars have been lost by the forces of good or bad customer service. One report issued by New Voice Media states that sixty-two billion dollars in 2016 was lost due to poor customer service. One theory that applies to such a loss is that "products are consumed, service is experienced." Experience is the factor that can influence a person's decision to either return or not return for the same service. Haven't you ever, in the process of waiting, had a bad experience that placed you in a bad mood? Didn't that mood cause you to lose the excitement or the enjoyment of what you were waiting for in the first place? Most people have a one-strike policy and will search for alternatives if the service experience was dreadful enough. We've all dealt with this.

Let's face it, our generation has acquired a certain perception on what is fair and how their time should be spent and respected. As a result, we have needed experts like the psychologists, along with mathematicians and engineers, to create a more pleasant experience while waiting in line or waiting for a service.

There are strategies that have been conceived over the years that offer companies a way to appease the customer that must wait for their service, such as managing expectations.

What do We Expect?

Popular restaurants that "pack the house" on the weekend understand how overwhelming it may feel when you step inside and see a lobby filled with a flock of hungry people waiting to be seated. As we approach the counter we just want to know one thing: how long will we have to wait? At this point, most restaurants have adopted customer service strategies and know that whatever expectation delivered to the guest will affect their experience. Let's say that I am told that the wait will only be forty minutes, even though they have personally calculated a time frame of thirty to thirty-five minutes. The brilliance behind this tactic is that I already agreed with a length of time that I am willing to wait; therefore, I lose my rights to complain if the expectation is met exactly as promised. If they play their cards right, I will be seated earlier—giving me this tremendous feeling that I received a victory. In my mind, I am ahead of schedule. My expectation was exceeded, and therefore I win! This is an example of influencing a person who had just waited quite a while to be served. In the psychology of waiting in line, that is how expectations are managed successfully.

In our world of faith, much of our frustration stems from thinking Jesus did not manage our expectations very well. We are unsatisfied "customers," ready to take our complaint to the person in charge. We've been waiting way too long in the lobby of life for our name to be called, and we are ready to walk. This is the common attitude that escalates when our expectations come with deadlines.

I am hoping by now in your journey, God has released promises over your life or several prophetic pictures of what He wants to do with you and for you. When these divine impressions enter our heart, our habit is to tally how long we think the process should take. We step into the danger zone of measuring what we think is a fair waiting time for God to bring to fruition what He had shown us. This way of thinking typically leads us to assume that God did not live up to His end of the bargain, leaving us embittered by His "performance." The truth is, you and I do not have permission to set the agenda and terms to His plan for us. God is not required to ever obey or abide to our theoretical schedule.

In the book of Acts the apostles, who were ready to take on the world for the cause of Christ, spent forty days after the resurrection receiving instructions from Jesus regarding the Kingdom. During that time, the scriptures acknowledge this question that the apostles constantly brought before Jesus.

> "Every time they were gathered together, they asked Jesus, "Lord, is it the time now for you to free Israel and restore our kingdom?" He answered, "The Father is the one who sets the fixed dates and the times of their fulfillment. You are not permitted to know the timing of all that he has prepared by his own authority."
> (Acts 1:6-7 TPT)

Sound familiar? The apostles were anxious to know times and seasons just as we are. And by the tone of this passage, it seems as though Jesus had to continually repeat Himself on this matter. Eventually, that curiosity had settled down, and the apostles were more focused on the work they were called to accomplish rather than when things would occur.

Making Promises

If we were to reminisce on the great stories of the Bible, we would recall God's promises to specific people chosen for His ultimate plan of redemption. For the promises to reach its full term depended entirely on the individual receiving the promise, for as it says in Romans 9:6 TPT: "Clearly, God has not failed to fulfill his promises to Israel, for that will never happen!" We can always count on God to fulfill His word; we are the ones who must learn to carry it through in the waiting.

A few mutual characteristics that can be seen when God would release a promise are:

1. The promise would always be so big and beyond what the person was capable of accomplishing.
2. The promise did not include a deadline or timespan.

Abraham received a mammoth-sized promise. With the obstacle of his wife physically "incapable of conceiving a child" (Romans 4:19 TPT), God promised Abraham that he would be a father of many nations and his descendants would be so many that they would be impossible to count. Medically, the promise was impossible because of their age, so each year would seem as though the promise was getting further and further away. Despite those facts, here's what we read about Abraham:

> "Against all odds, when it looked hopeless, Abraham believed the promise and expected God to fulfill it."
> (Romans 4:18 TPT)

Being that there was no "due date;" or a time limit to the promise, it was Abraham's faith in the waiting (an estimated twenty-five years) that was the key to the fulfillment of Gods plan.

> "So Abraham waited patiently in faith and succeeded in seeing the promise fulfilled."
> (Hebrews 6:15 TPT)

In most cases, when God has made a promise over my life, He instructs me to just believe until it is fulfilled. Even when the promise appears to be moving further out of reach, like it did for Abraham. This often allows His promise to test our promise. Our promise to follow His voice and to love Him without conditions; to love Him with all of our heart, soul, and mind.

Yes, there are prophecies and promises given to individuals that include a time-of-fulfillment stamp, but what you do is still a core part of the equation. If a prophet declares over an athlete that they will run in the upcoming Olympics four years from now, does the athlete play a part in that word? Would it be okay for the athlete to make less of an effort to train? After all—God promised, and His promises never fail, right? This example shows us we can work with or against the promises and prophecies of our lives. The four-year period would have arrived, and that unprepared, out-of-shape athlete would not make the team, simply because he did not do what he needed for the promise to be fulfilled. Time-sensitive prophecies are contingent to our response and to what we do in the waiting.

Jesus Himself did not know the appointed time for Him to experience the prophecies of His death and resurrection. He just knew God was faithful to complete what He had promised. In the realm of Heaven, over thousands of years, Jesus observed first-hand, the God of covenant fulfilling His word to man.

Otherwise, Jesus would have been pretty nervous about the entire cross ordeal.

Trust was never an issue for Jesus, which is why He could so easily say, "The Son is not able to do anything from himself or through my own initiative. I only do the works that I see the Father doing, for the Son does the same works as his Father" (John 5:19 TPT). Jesus had surrendered complete control over to the Father; obeying Him and resting in the assurance of His faithfulness no matter how bad things seemed to have gotten around Him. The trust we have in Him will always triumph over uncertainty.

Follow Me

Our first commitment is to Him and not the promise! Like a marriage proposal, Jesus has asked us to follow Him until the end. My covenant with my wonderful wife of twenty years is to be with her until the end. If we face health challenges, I'm there; financial hardship, I'm there; ministry restraints, I will be there. It is non-negotiable. My commitment is to her and not to what or when something will happen.

To this effect, Jesus invites us to follow Him and not the blessings of the Kingdom. We are told to seek Him first (see Matthew 6:33 NASB), and everything that is considered secondary will be added to us.

The apostles of old believed that Jesus would return any day. They believed the promise was for them during that era and eagerly anticipated His appearance. However, whether or not this would happen, their allegiance was to follow Jesus. On the heavier side of their journey, when persecution had caused them to be bound in chains, I'm sure they functioned in faith to believe God would free them and the length of their captivity did not intrude with their devotion to follow Him. Whatever happened in their lives, good or not so good, they followed Jesus.

In Acts chapter 21, Paul receives a prophecy saying he would be bound and handed over to non-Jews in Jerusalem. The close companions of Paul, in reaction to fear, anxiously attempted to persuade him not to go near Jerusalem. Paul replied:

> "Why do you cry and break my heart with your tears? Don't you know that I'm prepared not only to be imprisoned but to die in Jerusalem for the sake of the wonder of the name of our Lord Jesus?"
> (Acts 21:12 TPT)

How many of us would have the same "bring it on" bravado? How many of us would be ready to take on whatever unknown situation awaits us in order to follow the instructions of Jesus? I am not saying we should search for trouble, but I love the attitude and example Paul has left us.

Revealing My Heart

I think it best serves us to recognize who we are in times of struggle rather than to know who we are when experiencing great favor and victory. It is easy to rejoice when everything falls in to place and goes our way, but who we are when we are confronted with the challenges of life is who we need to know.

Peter had great intentions when he declared to Jesus that he would never deny Him, even if his life was being threatened (see Matthew 26:35 TPT). That same night, Peter aggressively denied Jesus on three different occasions. Peter did not know that was in him, but he sure needed to know. The entire scenario was to bring to light what Peter was capable of doing under pressure, all for the purpose of freeing him and not condemning him or his actions.

This passage in Deuteronomy provides us with a little more depth for this point.

> "You shall remember all the way which the Lord your God has led you in the wilderness these forty years, that He might humble you, testing you, to know what was in your heart, whether you would keep His commandments or not."
> (Deuteronomy 8:2 NASB)

God will place us in environments that deal with our heart. In the wilderness, the transitional holding place for the Israelites, God revealed their hearts as a gift. It is a grace gift for us to know our heart's response in various situations. Peter found the value of his exposed heart, whereas many people would have remained stuck under the failure of that act. By learning the true condition of his heart, he was able to make genuine adjustments that led him to be the pillar to which he was called.

Do not make the mistake of criticizing and condemning yourself when something about you has surfaced. Beating yourself up does not do you any good. Instead, cherish that knowledge and give your energy over to making that weakness into a strength. God Himself does not focus on our faults, but instead uses weak moments to redirect us to our potential. Peter was not reprimanded for his denial but was reminded, by Jesus, of who He had called him to be (see John 21 TPT). Jesus did not chastise Paul for his insurgent tactics against the Lord's followers. When they met at the road of Damascus, Jesus simply said, "Get up and go," (Acts 9:7 TPT) let's get you started, I have so much to show you.

Jesus could have gone down the long list of every one of Paul's offenses and dropped the shame hammer upon him because after all, Paul brought this on himself. Fortunately, that is not the character and disposition of our Messiah. He is there to root for you to rise when you fall and not rip you to shreds when you're down. Jesus will always have your best interest, and with that, you will sometimes need to discover what dwells in your heart—knowing the objective is your freedom.

Worthy of All

In the passage below, Paul admits that the Damascus road encounter could have gone another direction if he received what he deserved. He then credits the grace of God for rescuing him. In fact, Paul distinguishes God's grace as the very thing that has made him everything he has become.

> "Yes, I am the most insignificant of all the apostles, unworthy even to be called an apostle, because I hunted down believers and persecuted God's church. But God's amazing grace has made me who I am! And his grace to me was not fruitless. In fact, I worked harder than all the rest, yet not in my own strength but God's, for his empowering grace is poured out upon me."
> (1 Corinthians 15:9-10 TPT)

The worthiness of God's grace is the backbone of Paul's legacy. His ministry radically affected the entire world and Paul extends an invitation for us to be just as impacted. He tells all disciples to live their lives according to the worth of God's gospel of grace (see Philippians 1:27 TPT).

In the psychology of waiting in line, one conclusion presented was that waiting in line signifies our overall perception of a brand or service. If the consumer truly felt the quality of what they were waiting for was worth their time, their perception of a long line became more positive. They were willing to "do the time," because what they would receive in the end would not compare to the wait.

This mentality can be seen in the following scriptural example.

> "We view our slight, short-lived troubles in the light of eternity. We see our difficulties as the substance that produces for us an eternal, weighty glory far beyond all comparison, because we don't focus our attention on what is seen but on what is unseen. For what is seen is temporary, but the unseen realm is eternal."
>
> (2 Corinthians 4:17-18 TPT)

Paul shares his personal point of view because some Christians made their temporary, earthly trials so much bigger than some of our most momentous truths—such as the reality of our eternal inheritance. When we are able to grasp the heart attitude that Paul displayed in this passage, we too will consider our troubles as slight and short-lived compared to the lasting results that are ahead of us.

Anytime we perceive that what we are waiting for is well worth it, the length of time affects us much less. Another great example is with Jacob of the Old Testament who had fallen head-over-heels in love with a woman named Rachel and offered to serve her father seven years for her hand in marriage. Genesis 29:20 NASB says: "Jacob served seven years for Rachel and they seemed to him but a few days because of his love for her." The power of love and the power of what we value manages our experience in the waiting. I think it might be wiser for us to spend our time strengthening our love for Jesus and the ways of the

Kingdom, than to just focus on trying to strengthen our patience in the waiting.

Watch what will happen as you nurture a burning passion for the living God. That love will tangibly enforce the fruit of patience in a radical way. It did that with God, who believes you are worth His Son, and it will with us.

> "…the Lord is not late with his promise to return, as some measure lateness. But rather, his "delay" simply reveals his loving patience toward you, because he does not want any to perish but all to come to repentance."
>
> (2 Peter 3:9 TPT)

> "What is the value of your soul to God? Could your worth be defined by an amount of money? God doesn't abandon or forget even the small sparrow he has made. How then could he forget or abandon you? What about the seemingly minor issues of your life? Do they matter to God? Of course they do! So you never need to worry, for you are more valuable to God than anything else in this world."
>
> (Luke 12:6-7 TPT)

3
Save Me from Boredom

Legend has it, that the origin in forming a case-study category for waiting in the customer service arena began in the 1950's. The reported story took place at a high-rise office building in Manhattan where a great deal of complaints occurred regarding the excessively long wait for the elevator service. Tenants were becoming impatient, as they had to tolerate the inconvenient wait in the morning when they arrived, during their meal breaks, and, as they were anxiously ready to get on the road to head home. When the building manager realized that there was nothing he could technically do to cause the elevators to move any faster, he desperately turned to his staff to figure out a solution. During that meeting, several ideas were passed around in an attempt to relieve the people's frustration, but there was one proposal that was peculiar enough to consider trying. A daring team member suggested that they install floor-to-ceiling mirrors around the elevator area, with the intention of keeping the tenants distracted while they wait. As much as it seemed like a stretch, the gutsy staff went for it and the plan worked out brilliantly. The natural tendency for people to look at themselves and others while waiting kept them from being impatient, and the number of complaints amazingly dropped to nearly zero. To this day, elevators still use this method of diversion.

People who have nothing to do will always perceive wait times to be longer than those who are distracted or occupied. Taking that into account, businesses, airports, and waiting rooms of all sorts, have been providing time-fillers as a regular service, such as reading material, television screens, music, artwork, human interaction, and entertainment. All these diversions have played a major role in reducing the syndrome of restless customers.

Think of all the places that draw large crowds and large lines. For example, most theme parks have designed waiting in line as part of the experience. Disney has to be the reigning champion at this technique. You can bet that each ride is themed with interactive, fun-filled activities and visuals that will keep kids and adults happily occupied, without realizing they have been waiting in a forty-five-minute line for a four-minute ride. How we wait will always matter more than how long we wait.

Stay Active

When we do very little with our spiritual life, we can become antsy and bored. Boredom can instigate a world of trouble. As a teen, under the influence of a bored, aimless existence, I had my share of delinquent behavior. I stole from neighbors, I vandalized property, I experimented with illegal substances, and I engaged in a series of other devious acts.

My chaotic behavior and the route I was choosing emanated from the lack of purpose. Trouble found me because I did not know who I was, what I was doing, or where I was going.

Now imagine if I had lived out my days in complete consciousness of the Kingdom life, and I was occupied with a deep sense of purpose. I would not have had "room" for these distractive and destructive behaviors. One thing is for sure, if the body of Christ was aware of this purpose we would see a lot less gossip, backbiting, jealousy, competition, passivity, and complaining in the church. When you are occupied with one thing, it is hard to give attention to another. Nehemiah displays a perfect example for us. During his assignment to rebuild the walls of Jerusalem, a group of antagonists (who wanted the entire project to fail miserably) asked Nehemiah to come down from the wall and meet with them. His reply was a classic example of a man occupied with the will of God:

> "I am doing a great work and I cannot come down. Why should the work stop while I leave it and come down to you?"
> (Nehemiah 6:3 NASB)

Since Nehemiah had his eyes on the prize and on the goals of God, he did not allow any outside nonsense to have space in his life.

Open to Excuses

"Bored" is defined as feeling weary because one is unoccupied, or one lacks interest in their current activity.

When we think we have nothing to do but to wait, we can dangerously sink into a jaded reality that is desperately looking to find anything to occupy our life. We then open ourselves to experiences that will push biblical boundaries, just to temporarily "stimulate" the mundane cycle we have fallen into. Our excuse to our inaction is usually, "Once that prophecy rolls out and happens, then I'll do something." This excuse always implies that it is the "delay" of God that is keeping us passive. We say things like:

"I'm just waiting for God to provide the money. Once He comes through, then I am certain I will get more involved."

"As soon as the Lord opens wide the door that I'm waiting for, I'll make a move towards my calling."

Typically, this mentality causes us to do very little with our faith, because we are always waiting for something to happen before we swing into action. Biblically, that "something" will never show up because the principles of God will not bend. We must first be faithful over the little—the very thing He has given into our hands right now—before He makes the next move to give us the "something" more; the more that we are claiming to be waiting for in order to get in the game.

Occupy Until...

We were never meant to be still and just wait. Every day we have the wonderful opportunity to immerse ourselves in the things of God. Ephesians 5:16 TPT says:

> "...Take full advantage of every day as you spend your life for his purposes."

God is always saying and doing something that involves you. There is absolutely nothing boring about your life. You and I are born again citizens of the Heavenly realm with access to Heavenly resources. You are a chosen vessel clothed with power, love, and authority—geared to impact and influence the culture of today. There is so much more, but the greatest position and privilege of all is that we get to experience every day being a son and daughter to a loving Father. Your time of waiting for certain things to manifest does not ever have to feel stale or static, once you know what you have within you every day.

Sometimes we can confuse the passage that tells us to, "Be still, and know that I am God" (Psalm 46:10 NKJV) as a directive to be inactive until the thing you are waiting for arrives. Be still simply means we should surrender our anxiousness and cease from striving in our own effort; but it does not always mean to do nothing until...

One of the popular parables in scripture relays a pivotal message for all believers: Occupy with whatever I have given you, doing "business" until I return (see Luke 19:13 NASB). Jesus spoke this because the misconceptions of Him taking over Israel through a political movement had become a focus for His followers, and He needed to re-establish the daily priorities for the ones who would be future ambassadors of the Kingdom.

The parable began with a figure, who would represent Jesus, traveling from a province to take His rightful position as King. Before His departure, He called forth ten servants (the servants represent us) to be entrusted with a specific amount of resources while He was away. The servants were given the instructions to occupy their time by increasing the value of what they were handed to manage. When the King had finally returned from His journey, He summoned the ten servants to evaluate their productivity during His absence.

> "The first one came forward and said, 'Master, I took what you gave me and invested it, and it multiplied ten times.'
>
> "'Splendid! You have done well, my excellent servant. Because you have shown that you can be trusted in this small matter, I now grant you authority to rule over ten fortress cities.'

"The second came and said, 'Master, what you left with me has multiplied five times.'

"His master said, 'I also grant you authority in my kingdom over five fortress cities.'

"Another came before the king and said, 'Master, here is the money you entrusted to me. I hid it for safekeeping. You see, I live in fear of you, for everyone knows you are a strict master and impossible to please. You push us for a high return on all that you own, and you always want to gain from someone else's efforts.'

"The king said, 'You wicked servant! I will judge you using your own words."

(Luke 19:16-22 TPT)

In this parable, money is candidly a symbol of livelihood. In the natural realm, livelihood represents a means that secures the necessities of life. As a spiritual analogy, it represents any divine resource given to us for the sake of stewardship.

Through this parable we recognize that we are the King's servants, entrusted to occupy our time, by increasing in "size" whatever God has given us. We are to treasure what God has given us, big or small, and make the best use of it for His glory rather than complaining about what we were given to work with.

How we wait matters. The servants were largely rewarded by what they had done with their time while waiting for their King. In the eyes of the Master, Jesus, these are the ones that qualify to rule over greater opportunities in His Kingdom because they proved they were trustworthy in the small matters, which reveals another piece of the parable-puzzle. What the Master originally distributed to the servants was considered a small amount of resources, but that did not sway the Masters expectation for the servants to do something with what they had to work with. This leads me to a question: How do we find the inspiration to do something when what we have been given does not seem like much? I believe it highly depends on how we value what He presents to us. When our heart reigns with thoughts such as, "Is this all you're giving me Lord? How am I supposed to do anything with this?" then it is likely we will not do much with the little, forsaking the opportunity to experience more.

There are several stories of different people with entrepreneurial ideas who had been given a cash advantage of something like five thousand dollars. The ones that viewed this seed money as not enough never got their idea off the ground. Then there are other stories of people who embraced the amount given as a gift, foreseeing how they can use it to grow their idea, and as a result, multi-million-dollar brands were birthed. Vision and perspective is a big part of what we do with what we've been given.

Over the years, I have had little "coffee talks" with people who were struggling with personal issues and needed guidance. In our time together, I would offer advice that could propel them from their current grievances. As life went on, I've watched the ones that valued and received every foundational word in that short amount of time flourish and grow tremendously in character, strength, and faith. Some eventually became leaders in the church. They took that seed, nurtured and cherished it, and pulled every bit of power from those life-giving words. Others who had taken the advice lightly with a "that's it, Pastor?" attitude, are ones you'll find still circling around the same mountain. They did not multiply the "little" they were given.

If we do not value the little that God has given us, then the little will not have the chance to become much more.

Wicked

The parable concludes with a servant who had done nothing in the waiting with the resources given to him. This person was addressed as a "wicked" servant. The word wicked in this passage is used to describe someone who is morally wrong. Morals refer to principles of right and wrong behavior. They usually describe what is considered right according to the code of behavior of a particular society. The Kingdom of God is a society; a realm that has moral codes of what is considered right and wrong. With this in mind, I propose to you that the servant who did nothing had violated the code of that society. He was wicked because his behavior was wrong according to what is right. In Heaven's culture, it is wrong, wicked, and sinful to be passive, lazy, and negligent to the little that we have been given. Excuses do not cut it in the Kingdom. There is always something we can do.

Think about Nehemiah, who had a passion to rebuild the walls of Jerusalem to protect the remnant that had returned and to remove the shame of a city destroyed because of rebellion. At the time, Nehemiah was just a common slave, serving as a cupbearer in a faraway land. How would he pull off such a deed with these kinds of odds against him? He did not have any financial investors for this project, or the enormous amount of lumber needed to build a two-mile wall. He did not have governmental authorization, leadership experience, or even a team such as a construction crew that was able to support him and take on this massive, uphill-effort. So, what did he have? What did Nehemiah have to start with? The only thing he possessed was a deep desire and burden in his heart to do something for God and His people. That might seem "small" and powerless compared to the giant obstacles before him, but that burden turned into a day and night prayer and grew into a faith that overthrew the impossible.

IN THE WAITING

If you are familiar with the story, you know that eventually, every great need in this endeavor was favorably supplied. God has always been faithful to those who make no excuses but are faithful with whatever amount they have to start with. If an inexperienced, penniless slave can accomplish building this wall, what can you do with the little that you have?

Nehemiah is a glimpse on how God often operates. Most likely, God will make a promise or speak a prophetic word to you when your current life is nowhere near that word. You will look around at the condition of your life and think, "How is this ever going to happen?" When that day comes, if it has not already, do not get fixated on what you do not have, nor give in to the evaluation of how unqualified and unequipped you are for the vision placed before you. Instead, activate the core principles that were given to you in this chapter.

1. Value whatever it is you do have. However "little" it may seem compared to the big picture, and then guard it and grow it.
2. Remain faithful with the little. You may be serving in a very low-key position when the word over your life is to reach nations from a public platform. Whatever starting point God has for you, be faithful, and you will be guaranteed to one day experience the "more."
3. Stay occupied daily in Kingdom business. You'll never need to feel like you are just floating around, bored, and with nothing to do. God is always ready to engage in your life and create opportunities of growth and ways of reaching people around you.
4. Make no excuses. Do not fall in the victim cycle of, "When I have this, then I'll do that." You have all you need to be productive today.

5. Keep your faith-eyes on the prophetic words and promises no matter how outrageous the word might have seemed at the time. God loves to work against the odds.

These applications will ultimately attract the manifestation and the increase of what He originally presented to you. The dilemma is in the choice. You can allow the waiting to cause you to be inactive in your faith, only hoping something will change. Or you can occupy daily in the things of God, keeping yourself busy and fulfilled in the Father's will as you wait for the next breakthrough. The former choice will assuredly lead us to a spiritually stagnant, downward path and a vulnerable place of boredom.

What we do in the waiting is ultimately up to us. Might I suggest we take inspiration from the twelve-year-old Jesus who said this when His parents were searching for Him: "Did you not know that I must be about My Father's business?" (Luke 2:49 NKJV).

I urge you to occupy until you depart or the Lord returns. Take hold of this precious life, value the full length of your time, and be about your Heavenly Father's business, for then, you will assuredly behold the great things that take place in the waiting!

4
Weary in the Waiting

If we do not strengthen ourselves in the Lord, the process of waiting can make us restless and weary. When we become overwhelmingly weary, there is a threat to our faith walk. We are liable to give up things that are profoundly meaningful and valuable to us such as marriage vows, promotional opportunities, callings of God, Biblical priorities, and many other things that were once deemed precious. We can easily forsake and forfeit these things when we don't have the strength to continue and fight.

The enemy wants us tired because tired people give up. We stop caring. Once we are at the end of our rope, we tend to not care what we lose. In the history of sports, there have been championship-boxing tournaments where an opponent would call it quits in the middle of a title match because he or she did not have the physical strength to go on. These were fighters who have dedicated years to train for an opportunity to reign in their division; athletes who were highly competitive and desperately wanted nothing more than to win.

Are we not built the same? Are we not aiming to triumph in victory in every spiritual conflict that confronts us? We want to win! But what if, like the boxer, we feel as though we have nothing left to give in the battle? What do we do then?

Have you ever tried to inspire a friend to stand strong in the faith during a time when they were utterly fatigued and running on fumes by the challenging circumstance they were facing? I've had these encounters, and many of the "pep talks" have sounded like this:

> ME: "Do not give up, my friend. God promises that everything in your life will work out for good. If you would just hold on, God will redeem this situation with His relentless love, power, and grace. It will all certainly be worth it in the end."

> FRIEND: "It doesn't really matter anymore. It's basically over. I'm tired and I don't think I can last any longer."

> ME: "But there is such a significant calling on your life. It is so obvious. God has gifted you to do great and mighty things, and He will empower you with the divine strength you need to get through this. He loves you!"

> FRIEND: "I just don't have the passion anymore. I'm sure God can find someone way more qualified and stronger. The pressure is just too much for me."

We can become desensitized and closed off to the precious promises of God when our soul reaches a certain state of weariness. We start to not care about the very things we once considered worth fighting for, worth protecting, and worth pursuing. If we remain discouraged and worn down long enough without recharging, then the things we had once embraced as invaluable and indispensable to our life will slowly find its way to the graveyard.

I was unwell this week with the flu and was not able to get much of my usual work done. This is normally bothersome for me—because when my body is functioning at its best, I am prolifically active in my ministry assignments. As much as I love to be mobile and productive and knock out all my administrational tasks, none of that mattered when I was sick. I was weak and feeble and unable to be inspired. The way I felt physically and mentally, I did not care about any of my pressing deadlines. For a moment, I lacked interest in the things I am generally enthused about, because I was governed by a different me which was based on the decline of available energy in the natural.

In the spiritual context of things, we cannot afford to allow ourselves to get to that level where we just don't care, and we are saying, "Just take it, I give up, it's not worth it." That would be a catastrophe. Too many promises, dreams, destinies, and prophetic callings have been caught in the net of weariness.

Giving Up Our Birthright

Esau's story is one of the prime examples of how weariness can strip us from our destiny.

> "Now Jacob cooked a stew; and Esau came in from the field, and he was weary. And Esau said to Jacob, "Please feed me with that same red stew, for I am weary." Therefore his name was called Edom.
> But Jacob said, "Sell me your birthright as of this day."
> And Esau said, "Look, I am about to die; so what is this birthright to me?"
> Then Jacob said, "Swear to me as of this day."

So he swore to him, and sold his birthright to Jacob."

(Genesis 25:29-33 NKJV)

To ancient Rabbi's, Esau had become one of the most foolish and despised men in history on the grounds of this event. Some proof to this report is found by how the below passage uses Esau's folly as a warning to the body of Christ:

> "Be careful that no one among you lives in immorality, becoming careless about God's blessings, like Esau who traded away his rights as the firstborn for a simple meal."
>
> (Hebrews 12:16 TPT)

Before this caution statement occurred about Esau, the prior chapter parades a long list of champions of the faith, prompting us to walk in the shoes that these patriarchs have walked. Among this list, you will find men and women who were far from perfect. They were people who had committed acts of murder, adultery, and deception; yet they were praised for their heroic accomplishments in the realm of faith, while Esau was called out as the least likely person you would want to be. By giving up his birthright, Esau had violated the supreme moral of the Kingdom.

To the Jews, the birthright was the most sacred privilege in the family unit and the highest honor for a son. The firstborn became the priest of the household that would carry the family's name and everything the family stood for. He was handed the judicial authority of the father and allotted a double portion of the family's inheritance that was built and sustained by years of hard labor. This is what Esau had given up for a meager bowl of beans. In weariness, we are known to make very bad deals.

The birthright to us would represent everything we could

possibly be in Christ Jesus. Imagine, all that we have inherited through the sacrifice of the Savior we traded for a bowl of beans. No wonder Esau's name carried such a reputation. Never let the sacred become common and disposable when you are maxed out. The same way you grew weary, you can grow strong.

Growing Weary

> "Let us not lose heart in doing good, for in due time we will reap if we do not grow weary."
> (Galatians 6:9 NASB)

This passage reveals that none of us "get" weary, but we "grow" weary. In other words, your weariness did not happen overnight. The word grow means to increase in size or substance. This insinuates that weariness stems from allowing things to progressively build up, becoming larger and larger each day in our heart and mind. We all know that one negative thought can grow; it can increase in size if we give it enough daily attention. We do not just wake up one day and suddenly have a new mentality or a bitter heart. We do not suddenly become paralyzed with a fear of the future, plagued with self-doubt, or weary to the point of quitting. We grow, increase, and manifest into these things.

In the waiting, the enemy will whisper thoughts in attempt to get you to abandon your post and to trade in your divine calling for beans. We entertain thoughts like: "Is God even listening? Does He notice everything I am trying to do for Him? Why would I be placed in this situation if He loved me? It would probably be better if I would just give up and walk away, because it seems like it is just getting worse."

If we do not counter these types of thoughts with Kingdom truth, and they grow and echo in our heart and mind without any retaliation, we are bound to be weary and worn down in the waiting. We will lose heart while doing good and never possess the harvest that was planned for us. In essence, by your thoughts you can grow weary or you can grow stronger. The devil can wear you down if you accept his thoughts, or you can wear the devil down by resisting his thoughts.

> "So then, surrender to God. Stand up to the devil and resist him and he will turn and run away from you."
>
> (James 4:7 TPT)

In the Flesh

Without the Holy Spirit, we will have no strength to wait. Jesus said:

> "…As you live in union with me as your source, fruitfulness will stream from within you— but when you live separated from me you are powerless."
>
> (John 15:5 TPT)

Anytime we are operating from another source outside of Him and His Spirit, we are disconnected and powerless. The sad reality is that our natural human capacity and strength, formed in the flesh, is where many Christians function from while in the waiting. This is how we exhaust ourselves, even while doing good.

The Bible says a few things about living a life controlled by the flesh that should alarm us:

The mindset of the flesh will produce death to our identity and destiny (see Romans 8:6 TPT).

The mindset that is focused on the flesh fights against God's plan and refuses to submit to His direction (see Romans 8:7 TPT).

The flesh is a conflicting force that hinders the Holy Spirit from living free within us (see Galatians 5:17 TPT).

If you plant seeds of the flesh, you can expect to experience a harvest of corruption (see Galatians 6:8 TPT).

The flesh is weak (see Matthew 26:41 NKJV).

The flesh is untrustworthy, and we should place no confidence in it (see Philippians 3:3 NKJV).

The flesh will never pay off, it will profit us nothing (see John 6:63 NKJV).

The flesh does not have any defense against weariness. The flesh is weak, powerless, and unreliable. It is an empty investment that never pays out. The flesh attracts death and negativity and will always rebel and fight against the divine plans of God. It is not a good idea to just carry around a Christian badge, your salvation card, but be led by the flesh. You will eventually breakdown.

The good thing for you and me is that the Holy Spirit, who can do abundantly above whatever we can possibly think or ask (see Ephesians 3:20 NKJV), offers Himself to you at all times. In the waiting, the Holy Spirit will grace us with power that we never thought we had, in order to endure what would normally crush us. By walking under the influence and power of the Holy

Spirit, you are brought into a position to control the cravings and dominance of the fleshly self-life (see Galatians 5:16-17 TPT).

I do want to explore a great mystery that has meddled with the rational side of my mind for years. It is something that can only favor those who walk in the spirit. That is: When we are weak, we are actually getting stronger. It is almost like reaching the end of an hour-long workout, and your muscles hit that point of fatigue where you are unable to do any more lifting. You might feel weak at that time, but the truth is the workout actually made you stronger.

Weak but Strong

Here is a way that Paul put it:

> "And He has said to me, "My grace is sufficient for you, for power is perfected in weakness." Most gladly, therefore, I will rather boast about my weaknesses, so that the power of Christ may dwell in me. Therefore I am well content with weaknesses, with insults, with distresses, with persecutions, with difficulties, for Christ's sake; for when I am weak, then I am strong."
> (2 Corinthians 12:9-10 NASB)

Jesus personally spoke to Paul with a promise that His grace would be sufficient when he was feeling weak. To be sufficient is to be supplied with an ample and adequate amount for whatever need is at hand. We can rest in the fact that God's grace will always be sufficient enough to take on our insufficiencies. God's power is perfected in our weakness. We discover His strength and we can use that strength when we have none. Hours before

Jesus suffered at the cross, we find Him weary and weak and overwhelmed physically, mentally, and emotionally. In the peak of His prayer, Jesus—the bravest being that had walked the earth—uttered these words: "My Father, if there is any way you can deliver me from this suffering, please take it from me. Yet what I want is not important, for I only desire to fulfill your plan for me" (Matthew 26:39 TPT). Jesus was experiencing the weakest point He or anyone could humanly endure; yet He had the strength to undergo the cross. How is that possible? The Father's strength was sufficient enough for Him. He was very weak, yet He was strong.

Sufficient Strength

In 2004 my wife, Aury, and I were invited to minister in dance at a large church in Hawaii during their Sunday evening service. The pastoral leaders had asked if we could also share our testimony for a few minutes with the congregation at the end of our performance. Although we were a little nervous because we had never spoken in any capacity in front of a large group of people, we gladly accepted the opportunity.

On the day we were scheduled to minister, we were met with a few major challenges. Not only did I wake up feeling under the weather, but I also injured myself while rehearsing our duet. Somehow, in the midst of reviewing the steps, I severely strained my neck muscles, limiting the basic mobility I needed to dance. The degree of the discomfort was extreme, and I could barely move without grunting a painful squeal, let alone perform a high-energy hip hop routine. At that point, the wisest thing to do was to pass on the opportunity and that is exactly what I planned to do. However, God was up to something. Whenever I would get ready to inform the pastors my decision to decline, I felt a nudge—the whisper of the Holy Spirit—urging me to trust in the Lord, be patient, and watch what He does. Although I do not recommend for anyone to dance while injured, I just knew in that moment God was prodding me to function in a high level of faith. In my weakness, the Holy Spirit continued to encourage me to rely on the sovereign sufficiency of God's strength. Despite of the fact that there were no physical signs indicating that I would be healed as the day went on, I chose to hold on to the unction of the Holy Spirit.

The time had arrived for us to dance, but my neck was still stuck in the same critical condition. At that moment I thought, "Alright Lord, here we go. I am expecting something to happen. I don't know what it is, but I am trusting you." When the pastors introduced us, the church roared with expectation to see something special. The feeling was mutual. I was expecting something special as well. Aching with a motionless neck, I reluctantly began to ease my way towards my starting position for the dance, ready to give my best offering. Then it happened. As soon as I made contact with the stage, a supernatural surge went through my body and my neck suddenly loosened, rotating in circles, releasing me of all pain and stiffness. His strength had manifested over my weakness and I was able to do what I could not do.

The dance ended, and I was feeling amped from the phenomenal breakthrough. I was now earnestly ready to verbally minister for those few moments we were offered. Aury and I began to share briefly a summary of things God had been doing with us in the dance industry and our personal lives. As we were crossing over the five-minute time period we were allotted, I looked at the pastor and she cued us to go on a few more minutes. One revelation led to another and a few minutes turned into a few more minutes as the pastor kept gesturing to us to keep going. Without even consciously knowing, fifty minutes had passed and we ended up ministering the entire service. You have to remember, I had never preached at a church. This was the first time I experienced that anointing and discovered my gift of teaching that I never knew existed. My point is, had I not trusted in His strength during my weakened state, the beginning of the pastoral call (that I would eventually embrace) would not have kick started at that time. The results that came from that act of faith began a ripple effect that led us to start our church six years later.

Becoming Bigger

One of two things can take place when we are wrestling with something difficult that can cause weariness. God can either remove the burden or He can make you strong enough to carry it. For example, a construction worker that is new on the job might surprisingly find the heavy labor too difficult for him at the beginning. Does he ask his boss to reduce the workload or does he start to exercise so that he can get in shape and be strong enough to handle what is expected of him?

Should God take away every challenge we face, or should He supply us with strength to overcome the challenge? Should God disconnect us from all the difficult people in our lives, or should He unveil the power we possess to radically love those people beyond measure? He desires to show us who we truly are in Him.

God wants to make you bigger! Therefore, He does not always take away the "giants" before us, because He would rather unlock the giant-killer within us. To reign in life, we need God to reveal the greatest version of ourselves, to reveal the potential you and I are graced with. You are stronger, wiser, kinder, more patient, spiritually gifted, and more creative than you know. In many cases, it is in the waiting, in the weariness, where these strengths become visible.

"For our spiritual wealth is in him, like hidden treasure waiting to be discovered…"

(Colossians 2:3 TPT)

God Never Grows Weary

Here is the beauty of it all: We might become weary, but God never grows weary. If you step outside and begin to run with all of your might, you will eventually run out of human energy and have to stop (unless you're Forrest Gump). There is only so much we can do before we collapse. When it pertains to our God, Isaiah 40:28 NLT says: "He never grows weak or weary." His Spirit dwells inside every believer, which provides us each with an endless supply of strength and power, concluding that when we are weak, we can also be strong. The entrance into that strength begins with intimacy with God.

> "God, I'm so weary and worn-out, I feel more like a beast than a man.
> I was made in your image, but I lack understanding.
> I've yet to learn the wisdom that comes from the full and intimate knowledge of you, the Holy One."
>
> (Proverbs 30:2-3 TPT)

The passage implies that when we lack in the understanding of the full intimate knowledge of God, we are prone to become weary. But the deeper we abide in Him, the wider our strength capacity will become. Draw near to God and watch His strength draw near to you.

5
Face Forward

When it comes to a watching a football game, my wife, Aury, is far from patient. As thrilling as the sport may be to our American culture, it does nothing for her whatsoever simply because she does not get it. From her perspective, all she can see is a clump of big men charging towards each other only to topple to the ground and then repeat the same sequence.

What annoys her the most about the game is the time that it takes to run the next play. By comparison, she expects the players to be in constant motion equivalent to what you would see at a basketball or soccer tournament. Since she does not understand the technicalities of football and how it is vital to have those gaps between each play, she cannot conceive the reason why they are waiting, therefore she becomes impatient watching the game.

On the other hand, the waiting is exuberant for a super fan. The science and strategy that forms the next anticipated play captivates a true follower of the football league. But for someone that does not connect and understand the mechanics and process of the sport, waiting for the next action-packed play can be a big bore.

That is an example of how the process can lose its excitement when a follower of Jesus is unaware of the spiritual "strategy" that is infused in the waiting. This ignorance can lead us to feel like nothing is really happening and God is just letting time pass by without any objective taking place. That impression is false. Our God is highly involved in every part of our life. When He is silent, when He is loud, when things accelerate, and when things slow down, He is there permitting time to work on every part of us.

Now, if you let my wife have a full day to shop for fashion at a local mall, she will excel in patience. Even if she finds a blouse that she really likes, she will gladly invest the time to look around to get the best results. She will visit each and every retail establishment, covering the entire facility, to compare and explore her options before considering that purchase. Some men can feel my pain.

Why Wait?

When we do not have much interest in the very thing we are supposed to be patient to receive, or we fail to comprehend the significance or reason to wait, then a few minutes can feel as though we are caught in a slow-motion action excerpt. On the contrary, if we are given something we can visually grasp and perceive as worthy to invest time, then we will happily endure the duration needed for it to manifest. We will wait much more steadily and sternly when we can see the purpose ahead.

> "When there is no clear prophetic vision, people quickly wander astray…"
> (Proverbs 29:18 TPT)

Without seeing something ahead of us, waiting will seem like time is passing in vain. If there is not a prophetic vision for the future pushing us forward, we will ultimately digress in our journey and wander from the course divinely carved out for us. Who would ever want to get in a car just to drive in circles? That would be insanity. We'd rather have a target, a clear destination. Even if we are delayed by traffic or detours, at least we are heading somewhere and there is a purpose to our trip.

Picture a man who is living in poverty and has just received news that he has inherited a hundred thousand dollars from a family member. The only condition to this transaction is that he would have to wait for a period of one year before he can collect this gift. Although the funds are detained for a moment, life just got better for him. He might still be in his circumstance, wearing the same tattered garments, managing the same difficulties that lack creates, but joy and hope has struck this man, because every day is a step closer to a better outcome in life. That is what vision does; it shows us that where we are now is not where we are staying, because we are heading to a destination.

Many things can occur in the waiting. Things like reconstructing our faith muscles, training our hands for war, shifting the priorities of our heart, stripping us from natural resources to trust His, developing promised-land level character, freeing us from religious thought patterns, or simply drawing us into deeper waters of intimacy with Him. Whatever things are taking place; it is transportation to a purpose. God always has a future in mind for you (see Jeremiah 29:11 NKJV), and He is building a bridge to get you there.

When we perceive the opposite and presume that God is holding us back without any cause or reason, we run the risk of resenting that we ever trusted Him in the first place. This is the unfortunate outcome for many in the body of Christ who suppose that God has brought them to a dry and dingy waiting place without any destination. This is never the truth and we should fervently guard our hearts from any thoughts that agree with this deception. Always remember, the most important thought you'll ever have is your thought towards God. In fact, the greatest goal we should desire to reach in the process of waiting should be that our relationship with God has grown deeper and stronger.

Forward

Perception is everything. How we see and interpret every situation, what we believe as truth and our reality, will determine our every move in the waiting. Do you have a vision of your future that is beyond your current circumstance?

A woman expecting a child knows the standard nine months of pregnancy leads to birthing a new life. With that in mind, while carrying she will make changes that accommodate the arrival of her newborn. It is very likely that a room will already be built and decked-out with furnishings that suit the infant's instinctual needs. Some moms have even been known to begin a college fund before the child is born. We will always prepare for what we anticipate and what we see coming towards us in the future.

I firmly believe that when we are put in a position to wait and be patient, it is because God is birthing something in us and from us. From prophecy conceived to prophecy fulfilled, you are being prepared to give birth to a God-ordained vision. You are feeding something, carrying and strengthening a call, and incubating a purpose, in order to give it life one day.

Every principal character in scripture that carried and gave birth to a promise from God, was only able to survive and endure the process by keeping the vision fresh and their face forward. The Lord knows we will always move towards what we see, so we are expected to fix our eyes on a future hope. It was the only way our forefathers waited decades to give birth to what seemed impossible at the time of conception.

Living face forward was the fundamental strategy that kept the apostle Paul advancing in the calling of God amongst intense persecution. Here is what he wrote to the Philippian church on this subject:

> "...I run with passion into his abundance so that I may reach the purpose that Jesus Christ has called me to fulfill and wants me to discover. I don't depend on my own strength to accomplish this; however I do have one compelling focus: I forget all of the past as I fasten my heart to the future instead."
> (Philippians 3:12-13 TPT)

This forward, future-minded focus is a staple in the scriptural life for believers. For example, God instructed Lot's family not to look back when they fled from the destruction of Sodom, and Jesus had pronounced a protocol for those wanting to be His disciple:

> "Jesus responded, "Why do you keep looking backward to your past and have second thoughts about following me? When you turn back you are useless to God's kingdom realm.""
> (Luke 9:62 TPT)

My Darkest Hour

Forward thinking and forward seeing is imperative in the waiting. We must always have a vision looking to the future. I personally would not have lasted in the darkest days of my life unless I believed with all my heart that God is good and there was a hope beyond my circumstance. Here is my testimony taken from my first book, *Living Souled Out*:

When we launched our church in 2010, everything seemed to go as planned. Core values were established, the vision of who we are as a church formed, and we did whatever we could to create a drama-free culture. We desired to be as simple as possible, yet fully effective—and that is what we began to witness each week. In my estimation as a pastor, everything was perfect—until we hit the six-month mark after our grand opening. That is when I was summoned to confront the greatest challenge of my life.

Traditionally, my wife and I relax on Sunday night after an exhausting day of serving at the church. We usually start off our "zone-out" session by indulging in comfort food, and then we spend the rest of the evening watching a flick or catching up on some television shows we recorded during the week. On one particular Sunday night, while unwinding in my customary slouched position, I felt this shadowy, overwhelming presence swaddle me like a blanket until it literally took over all my senses and natural ability to think. I suddenly found myself lost in a world of darkness as everything closed in, and my thoughts were uncontrollably not my own. I recognized this was an anxiety attack; a mental tornado of destructive thoughts aiming to wreck any kind of functional reality. I leaped out of my seat in search for some relief from the fear looming over my being. I began to shake as if possessed (which is what it felt like). My wife freaked out for a split second at the sight of her husband helplessly convulsing. Then she dove into a charismatic frenzy, rebuking every demonic spirit in the book that she's ever heard of.

It is hard to imagine the feeling I'm attempting to describe unless you have been a victim of this type of experience. I had struggled through a few anxiety attacks ten years before this event and had been freed from the condition through Christ, up until that moment. This time was different. The scale of the anxiety was substantially more intense, and unlike the former attacks that had lasted around ten minutes, this one did not stop for nearly four long months. This torment would mercilessly envelope me literally twenty-four hours a day. Obviously, the attack had been mapped out by the ruler of darkness with the intent of destroying the head of a new church. This was not a hidden agenda, as the demonic figures made themselves perfectly known. I could often see their bodily figures move around me when they visited. Several times a day I would hear satanic voices advising me to take my life. They would attempt to convince me that I would never be delivered from this torturous existence. They insisted that standing my ground for Christ was a big waste of time because Jesus did not care about my situation. The fact is, it certainly seemed that way. I hardly felt any sort of presence or comfort from the Lord during that time, nor did He speak to me intimately as I once had known. It honestly felt as though God had completely abandoned me.

I thoroughly examined my life and checked for "opened doors," hidden sin, or negative seeds I might have sown. I think I forgave everyone I've ever known a hundred times, from childhood bullies to people whose names had slipped my mind. I turned over every rock and microscopically searched the condition of my heart. I desperately did everything I could on my end, but none of it eased my agony. Indeed, the pain only got worse. If I had not known this was a spiritual battle, I would have declared myself clinically insane and checked into a mental facility. I was a mess. I could not sleep, eat, or focus in any normal capacity. It looked as though I was losing an endless battle, fatally declining in this death match.

I had a choice. I could look at how darkness was dominating

my entire existence while God appeared to be absent, or I could trust in everything I'd ever believed about Jesus, in spite of the ongoing nightmare I was living. The question at hand was: "Do I believe everything I've sung on Sundays, read in scripture, or confessed about God as a Christian for the past fourteen years, or was I just 'playing church' the entire time?" I decided to believe. I chose to trust God.

I would repeat to Him, "I love you and I know you love me. I will serve your Kingdom, even if this is my reality, my thorn, for the rest of my earthly life." I never spoke one word against God but instead offered a tribute of praise to Him around the clock. In the middle of the night, when my sleep was interrupted, I danced. In my weakness, I worshipped in dance with all my might until my frail vessel had nothing else to give. Every Sunday I stood before my church family and ministered, with zeal, the heart of Jesus without broadcasting my predicament. I refused to withhold my love, adoration, and service from my faithful King and Messiah. I had meant every single word when I proclaimed a covenant with Jesus years ago, stating my commitment to live "souled out" for Him. My expressed devotion was never a conditional promise. It was always set up to be for better or worse, through the good times and—yes—even the bad.

Eventually, the anxiety lifted, and I was free! When I ponder that experience, I celebrate the work that was accomplished. Though I understand it was not God who authored the incident, He used every bit of that fire to make gold.

Hope is Here

I share this experience to testify of the power of vision. As I was attacked with a constant, relentless barrage of death thoughts and destruction, I could see something beyond the chaos and confusion.

I was able to see in the depths of my heart that He is a good God, a God that had a promising future packaged and designed just for me. If I had no vision in my weakest, most wearisome moment, I would have drowned in a hopeless pit without a path to escape. It would have been over for me and the ministry assigned to my life. Instead, I did whatever I could to muster at least one godly, hope-filled thought towards my destiny every single day.

Vision was my lifeline that kept my head above water. It gave birth to the ministry opportunities that my wife and I are now experiencing. The beauty of giving birth and moving from process to promise is that you are able to detach from the pain, by the joy that springs forth in the new level you have entered.

> "Just like a woman giving birth experiences intense labor pains in delivering her baby, yet after the child is born she quickly forgets what she went through because of the overwhelming joy of knowing that a new baby has been born into the world."
>
> (John 16:21 TPT)

Lead Me to Me

The future tells me my action for the present and who I need to be now. A baby on the way indicates to the mother-to-be who she must become and what she needs to change in her life today. If there is a prophetic word calling me to entrepreneurship, to employ hundreds that would take the reins of social justice issues, then I need the waiting time to begin to develop me into that leader now.

Recently my wife and I had lunch with a young couple, James and Shaylen, who are in their early thirties. They shared a vision on how God has called them to make a dramatic difference in this generation by occupying governmental positions that would influence the educational system. I was thrilled to hear the depths of their plan, but most of all, the time they were willing to commit for this to be fulfilled. James would be around sixty years old when the final steps of this vision would unfold. Although this section of their career-calling would not be for many years to come, this future vision is ordering every step they are taking today. Every prophetic vision should speak to our present.

The greatest example of all is the crucifixion of Jesus. To endure the cross, He pictured humanity, a people whom He loved free from the curse and bondage of sin (see Hebrews 12:2 TPT), reconciled to the Father. That vision was language to Jesus. It spoke to Him through every agonizing beating. "This is painful, but I can see a people I consider worthy of this sacrifice, I envision mankind redeemed to their original position and identity, I can see the will of My loving Father fulfilled." Through every miserable moment, Jesus had to see the ultimate plan of God, or He would have crumbled and not have endured. He became the Savior He needed to be in His darkest hour, because a vision of the future was present in His mind.

When you can see it, you will be able to wait for it.

> "…because our hope is set on what is yet to be seen, we patiently keep on waiting for its fulfillment."
> (Romans 8:25 TPT)

> "This vision is for a future time. It describes the end, and it will be fulfilled. If it seems slow in coming, wait patiently, for it will surely take place. It will not be delayed."
> (Habakkuk 2:3 NLT)

6

The Making of a Masterpiece

I never planned or desired in any shape or form to become a pastor, or anyone for that matter who would teach the Bible in front of a crowd. Growing up, my absolute greatest fear was speaking in public. Even the idea of verbally expressing myself before peers in a small group terrified me.

In high school, I was enlisted to take a Speech class. Yes, you guessed it, it was not just a course to teach you how to write a speech, but you would eventually need to orally conduct a presentation. I braved the "dare" and saddled up to conquer glossophobia, my speech anxiety, thinking that this has held me back way too long and I should be able to stomp all over it by now. After all, there was only one final exam where we would need to speak on our own, so it should not be so bad. If I can just knockout a swift five-minute expedition, then the nightmare will be all over. I would quickly be out of the spotlight, just like ripping off an old Band-Aid. No problem, right? Well, not quite. The day my teacher announced that we would need to speak before the class as our final assignment, the bold, valiant, and gutsy attitude had ditched me, and I was back to square one of being paralyzed with fear and imagining every embarrassing possibility. Though the class consisted of only thirty students, it felt like a sea of censuring eyes would soon be watching and critiquing my every move. The fear was so consuming and intense that I entertained the thought of taking a failing grade and just deal with the consequences.

I made my intentions known to my instructor, who surprisingly expressed a deep compassion for my issue, and actually allowed me to team up with another classmate. Though I was highly favored to be the only student sharing the stage with another, I still found myself in a world of turmoil, scared out of my wits. I think I had human pity working on my side, but my gracious teacher was flexible enough to allow another compromise. My fellow student ended up doing the entire speech on his own and all I did was mime his words; physically demonstrating the presentation without uttering a sound. To this day, I still do not know how I passed Speech class without having to literally speak.

Fast-forward to my life today, I am a pastor who speaks publicly in front of hundreds of people on a regular basis. This is something I, or anyone who knew the old me, would have never predicted. It is typical for the Lord to use the waiting to reconstruct and utterly transform our lives; to have us do things we never imagined we'd be doing.

A Masterpiece

Many of my principal leaders, that I have the pleasure of serving alongside with in the Kingdom, have initially walked through the church doors with a life that was in disarray. There were no visible, external signs whatsoever that would make you think they would influence and impact culture at the capacity they do today. Several of my leaders arrived at an all-time low in their life, caught in a web of darkness, depression, and suicidal tendencies. They had become a product of their dysfunctional settings that were void of stability and affirmation. Ultimately, these negative environments contributed to their shattered self-images and frequent fits of self-hatred.

When my leaders share their stories of the past and describe the destructive behavior that had become their standard way of life, they feel as though they are speaking about someone else. They find it difficult to even identify with that person of the past, because a shift in the spiritual paradigm had so radically turned everything around.

This is the brilliant handiwork of God. In the waiting, He takes the blight, broken, disfigured pieces of clay from our former life to manifest a beautifully divine masterpiece (see Ephesians 2:10 NLT). As a pastor, I experience so many people who stand at the outskirts of intimacy with God, thinking they have to clean up before they draw near to Him. They fear that God will not receive them in their complicated, unruly mess of a life—not knowing that He is the God that races towards the rebellious, prodigal believer, only to smother them with kisses (see Luke 15:20 TPT).

I love what Paul wrote to the church to remind us that it is God who takes our common, pedestrian lives and makes it masterfully shine. He wrote:

> "Brothers and sisters, consider who you were when God called you to salvation. Not many of you were wise scholars by human standards, nor were many of you in positions of power. Not many of you were considered the elite when you answered God's call. But God chose those whom the world considers foolish to shame those who think they are wise, and God chose the puny and powerless to shame the high and mighty. He chose the lowly,

the laughable in the world's eyes—nobodies—
so that he would shame the somebodies. For he
chose what is regarded as insignificant in order to
supersede what is regarded as prominent."

(1 Corinthians 1:26-28 TPT)

It is very common for God to release prophetic dreams and visions, words of knowledge and thoughts of destiny that might not resonate with the person you are today. You may not be anywhere near the great things you hear Him calling you into, but that is perfectly normal and beautiful because the greater the transformation, the greater the glory.

Choosing His Disciples

As a Rabbi, Jesus could have chosen young students of the law to be His disciples. In fact, no other Rabbi has ever enlisted a group of disciples that did not graduate from the educational system created for the up-and-coming religious leaders.

In the Jewish culture of Jesus' day, every Hebrew boy began their schooling at the Bet Sefer (House of the Book) at the age of six. In order to pass and move on to the next level of training, the student needed to study and memorize the entire Torah (the first five books of the Bible). If you were able to accurately quote, word-for-word, each book successfully, then at age eleven you would continue your educational journey to the Bet Talmud (House of Learning). If you failed to complete the strict, standard requirement of repeating these books verbatim, you were automatically disqualified and excused from the ministry. You were told to return home and learn a trade from your family such as farming or fishing, because the opportunity to become a minister has ended.

You might have already guessed that the majority of the students did not make it to the next level. The task was nearly impossible. Imagine trying to memorize every word from the last novel you read, and if that was not hard enough, imagine making that effort as an elementary school student. The purpose for such a severe guideline was to weed-out those they believed did not have what it took to be an elite religious teacher and representative of Israel. They only welcomed the best of the best, the cream of the crop.

The finest and most competent students went on to fulfill the next stage of their education by enrolling in the Bet Talmud, a school that would push the mental boundaries even further. It was mandatory for these pre-teen pupils to memorize the rest of the Hebrew Bible and master the Jewish art of question and answers. The very few students that had accomplished the demands of the Bet Talmud and graduated at the age of fourteen, moved on to the final phase of the Bet Midrash (House of Study).

At this level, you would present yourself before the esteemed Rabbis of that day, waiting for them to say these coveted words: "Come, follow me." This meant, "Come and be my disciple; take my yoke; learn and replicate my entire set of beliefs and core interpretation of the scriptures."

For a Rabbi, selecting a disciple was one of the most important choices he had to make. He would want the very best scholarly protégé to represent his legacy in the community. Therefore, the Bet Midrash was the only option in finding someone qualified—until Jesus came along.

Jesus recruited twelve men your traditional Rabbi would never consider drafting into their fold. He chose a handful of fishermen, which were in essence, Bet Sefer dropouts and had been told that they were not qualified for ministry and would have to settle for a family trade. Jesus also chose one of the most despised sinners in society, who was a traitor and cheat to his own countrymen: Matthew the tax collector. Let's not forget Simon the Zealot—a man who was a part of a radical political movement that incited the people to rebel against the Roman government.

These were the mix of people, the misfits of the world, that Jesus had elected to bring the Kingdom of Heaven to Earth. He could have chosen the conventional route and handpicked the most brilliant, top-grade apprentices, who were specially trained to be spiritual leaders, and who have thoroughly proven themselves to be experts in the study of God's word. Instead, Jesus went against the grain, and gathered the underdogs of life.

Sometimes I picture the high profile Rabbis of that time touring the city with their entourage of prestigious students, fresh from the Bet Midrash; and here comes Jesus, stepping into the scene with His unusual, rugged, spiritually untamed, motley crew—there to represent the Son of God and change the world. What a sight!

Jesus was not ashamed to be seen with His chosen vessels and He is not ashamed to walk with us from the bottom of our pit, to the top of our destiny mountain. He loves to take what the world rejects, tosses aside, and disqualifies, and create a signature masterpiece. Jesus is truly the author and finisher, founder and perfecter of our faith (see Hebrews 12:2 NKJV). Give God, the Master builder, a chance and watch what He can do with you in the waiting.

Becoming Like My Teacher

The main emphasis of waiting is not to become a more patient being, but to learn to be like Jesus.

"A disciple is not above his teacher, but everyone who is perfectly trained will be like his teacher."

(Luke 6:40 NKJV)

The relationship between a teacher and student was perceived much differently than how it is comprehended today. Our modern way of viewing someone becoming "perfectly trained," is based on the amount of information they consume and add to their foundation of knowledge. Whereas, the Biblical model is fulfilled by the disciple becoming transformed into the nature of their teacher and completely embodying their Rabbi.

The disciples training went way beyond your basic pen-and-pad knowledge. They would need to observe and echo every single aspect of their teacher's life. From their style of speech, to their eating habits, and even down to their bathroom etiquettes. There was nothing off limits when it came to emulating their teacher. If the Rabbi had a leg injury and walked with a slight limp, the disciples that were training under him would also walk with a limp.

This might seem a little bizarre and over-the-top, but the intention was pure. The student had one main goal, which was to reach the point where you could not tell the difference between him and his teacher.

Similarly, our objective as modern day disciples is to incarnate Christ and to personify the nature, heart, and disposition of our Savior. This way we get to know Him more, and He becomes visible to the world. Our aim as a Christian is not to fill our minds with knowledge about Jesus, but to become Jesus by transfiguring into the image of Christ.

Jesus manifested God on the Earth. He told His disciples, "He who has seen Me has seen the Father" (see John 14:9 NASB). Paul said to the Jesus community that they should imitate him just as he has been imitating Christ (see 1 Corinthians 11:1 NKJV). These examples model the epitome of our divine call; for us to one day say, "If you've seen me, you've seen Jesus."

Let's read this dialogue from Jesus after He had clothed Himself as a house-servant to wash the disciples feet:

> "You've called me your teacher and lord, and you're right, for that's who I am. So if I'm your teacher and lord and have just washed your dirty feet, then you should follow the example that I've set for you and wash one another's dirty feet. Now do for each other what I have just done for you. I speak to you timeless truth: a servant is not superior to his master, and an apostle is never greater than the one who sent him. So now put into practice what I have done for you, and you will experience a life of happiness enriched with untold blessings!"
>
> (John 13:13-17 TPT)

Jesus was saying to His disciples that they can call Him Teacher and Lord as much as they want; but if He indeed held these positions in their life, they would do exactly what He did.

A Different Person

In 1 Samuel chapter ten, the prophet Samuel had privately anointed Saul and appointed him to be the first ruler of Israel. Samuel then shared that as Saul would travel back to his home-base, he would meet a band of prophets and experience a divinely inspired transfiguration.

"...the Spirit of the Lord will come powerfully upon you, and you will prophesy with them. You will be changed into a different person."

(1 Samuel 10:6 NLT)

When Saul received the prophetic promise of kingship, he remained the same, timid person that he was before. It was not until the Spirit overtook him and invaded his inner being that the nature of Saul completely transformed.

We do not undergo any supernatural alteration by simply receiving a public promotion, a new title, or recognition and praise from man. We can only become a different person by the Spirit of God. When we open ourselves to be molded by the Holy Spirit that dwells within each believer, our lives drastically change. Who you are today can be completely different from who you can be tomorrow. With God, there is always more.

It Takes Time

Our lives are not forgotten in the waiting; they are formed. It takes time to create a masterpiece. Several years ago, Aury and I were hired to choreograph for a film that was shot in Paris, France. We were there for nearly six weeks, which gave us plenty of free time to explore the city as tourists. One of the fondest memories during our sightseeing trips was walking through the beautiful cathedrals. These magnificent architectural monuments featured the most stunning hand-carved sculptures that eyes can see. I thought it was profound that it took over two hundred years to build these historical structures, meaning that the original visionaries were not alive to see the completion of their masterpiece. They knew beforehand that if the constructional artistry were to be done right, it needed time.

It will take patience and process and time and labor to transform into the superior, upgraded version of our selves. There are some things we inherit by faith—free of charge, and without any hidden fees, such as grace and salvation; but the person we become in the waiting is a costly endeavor. The trials, transitions, and testing all come with a price. This can be difficult for a generation who wants maximum results with minimum effort. We love instant returns and rewards.

You can't blame the millennial mind when such words as high speed, express service, fast, and quick is embedded in the culture of our Western society. This is why you will rarely receive a positive reaction to these foundational words that are found everywhere in the pages of scripture:

Patience
Endurance
Perseverance
Faith
Hope

These words of waiting are important words, but they usually do not translate well for a people who habitually stare at the final seconds of the microwave. Think about all the lifestyle products that once dazzled the public for moving at groundbreaking speeds that we now criticize for its sluggish performance.

I remember what was considered a luxury to have during my mid-twenties. We had at-home answering machines instead of instant messages. The television shows we missed were recorded on videotapes with a limited amount of space, unlike the direct downloads that can be watched anywhere, anytime. Before you can enjoy your vacation highlights that you captured on camera, you needed to take that film to your local market and wait days for it to be seen.

IN THE WAITING

Technology is rapidly changing, and it will continue to expand and advance while hitting record speeds in this competitive market. Nevertheless, the principles of the word and the process for each believer will remain constant. No matter how "instant" our world gets, the waiting will still be a part of every disciple who is becoming transformed to reflect the nature of their Messiah Jesus.

Be ready for change and submit to the process, because God is creating a wonderful masterpiece in you!

7

A Storm-Proof Foundation

I remember many years ago, I ran into an old friend from high school at the church I was attending. I had just become a believer and I thought it would be exciting to walk this new path with someone I knew from my "former life." Aside from accepting Jesus as her Savior, this was a good time for my friend to welcome Jesus in her life as she was dealing with the fresh wounds of a divorce and financial challenges.

The following Sunday we made contact again in the lobby and I can tell by her countenance that she was unsettled and flustered about something. She briefly shared how she was involved in a minor car accident that week and then expressed these final words as she was exiting the building: "I thought everything in my life would be better now that I am going to church."

She left in haste that day and never returned, disappointed that her new-found faith did not live up to her expectation. She gave God seven days to make her life "better." The truth is, God did make it better the moment she gave her heart to Jesus. I think having every one of our sins forgiven and being accepted and adopted into an eternal family with God is quite an improvement. Life is certainly better with Jesus. You cannot ask for a better gift.

But as for my friend, she translated a "better life" as nothing bad will ever happen to her again, not even a mild fender bender.

Not an Option

Becoming a faith-filled, spirit-led, believer in Jesus does not keep us away from problems. We are not immune to the difficulties people face; we just now have an advantage over these problems. With Jesus, we are thoroughly equipped and empowered to overcome every trial, every temptation, and every test. Jesus did say that in this world we will experience trouble and sorrows, but because of the peace He possessed in Himself will now be in us, we can tackle the nuisance of life without losing our way or sacrificing our joy (see John 16:33 TPT).

Shouldn't our reflexive response to life's adversities be one of the major things that set us apart from the world anyway? Our life should resemble the same faith in affliction, the same calm in calamity, and the same trust in trouble that Jesus had. For our spiritual life to truly progress, our focus has to be less about what happens to us, and much more about our reaction, recovery and comeback. We will all likely encounter an occasional punch in the gut, slap in the face, and stab in the back from life—but we can always rise.

> "For the lovers of God may suffer adversity and stumble seven times, but they will continue to rise over and over again."
> (Proverbs 24:16 TPT)

That was the story of the apostle Paul's life. He refused to stay down. Though persecution would frequently follow him, as it did for all those who pioneered this movement, Paul remained a pillar for the Lord. The next passage will give you an idea of his personal perception that made the man unstoppable.

> "Though we experience every kind of pressure, we're not crushed. At times we don't know what to do, but quitting is not an option. We are persecuted by others, but God has not forsaken us. We may be knocked down, but not out."
> (2 Corinthians 4:8-9 TPT)

Paul created a perpetual resilience, an endure-all mentality, based on one inherit attitude—quitting is not an option. If he was down, the only option available in his book was to get back up, recover his strength, and regain momentum to move full-steam ahead. As a matter of fact, this stance was seen on his very first missionary journey. Jews who opposed Paul instigated crowds to stone him and then drag his body outside of the city to be left for dead (see Acts 14:19 TPT). When Paul miraculously stood to his feet (from the dead or near-death, I'm still uncertain), he immediately went back into the city to complete his gospel-invasion assignment (see Acts 14:20 TPT). From the very beginning of his ministry, Paul made it clear that he was not going to be stopped.

The idea of quitting can only exist if a reason for quitting exists. Paul took care of that by eradicating any type of grounds for walking away because there was only one way, one truth, and one life for him—and that was Jesus (see John 14:6 TPT). Living with one option was also a distinctive trait of his Messiah, Jesus. He often said, "I can ONLY do what the Father tells Me" (see John 5:19, 5:30, 8:28 TPT). The fact is, Jesus was not a robot and could have done whatever He wanted to do. But in His mind, there was not another option. Likewise, serving Jesus until his very last breath was the only possible choice for Paul, regardless of the trials he would face or the triumphs he would taste. You could say that this was his foundation and the permanent position he planted himself all the days of his life.

Don't be Surprised

The stronger the foundation the steadier our stand. We know we can hold our natural, physical "balance" longer if we stood on a solid, smooth, cement surface than on a flimsy, unstable one. It is the same concept with the spiritual world and our inner being. That is why my friend from high school only lasted two Sundays and a car accident before she departed from the faith. Whereas, you see men like Richard Wurmbrand endure fourteen years of imprisonment with torture by a Communist regime only to become more faithful to the cause of Christ.

The life that is set before every believer contains obstacles. It should not be a shock to our system when we occasionally encounter difficulties. Peter said it himself when he wrote to the church:

> "Dear friends, don't be surprised at the fiery trials you are going through, as if something strange were happening to you."
> (1 Peter 4:12 NLT)

Were we not introduced to life this way? From crayons to college, we learned that in order to advance in the educational system from one level to another, we need to successfully conquer the challenges of each course. This concept is in our instinctual DNA. It is not a surprise. It is even being ingrained in our video games; if you defeat the monster in each difficult stage, you move on to the next level. That is what makes gaming so much fun for the masses—the challenge is what gives them a chance to advance.

Foundations and Storms

The temptation in the waiting is to see the challenges as something preventing us from our calling—when in reality; the challenges propel us towards our calling. As long as we have a firm foundation keeping us steady in the storm, we will just keep getting bigger and better. On the opposite end, when we do not have a firm foundation, we live on a downslope and eventually get worse rather than better.

I once had to confront a friend who served in several key areas of the church. Although he was seasoned in the work of ministry, he had several episodes of outburst and his immaturity was only escalating. When we sat down to resolve these issues and to find healing and freedom, the one thing he articulated as a justification to his behavior was, "I have been doing ministry and church for a long time and that is why I am like this." That statement summed up his internal philosophy: The longer we serve the Lord, the worse we will all eventually become. He believed his actions were perfectly acceptable because the typical tendency for a Christian is to migrate to a bitter, impatient, and passive state along the way. My rebuttal was that the longer we are with Him, the better we should become. I believe being properly exposed to Jesus on a well-maintained foundation increases our zeal and zest for the Kingdom. We are more joyful and jubilant, loving and compassionate; and yes, we are more patient and content. I understand we will have days where the dynamics of spiritual warfare is intense, and we feel weak and uninspired. But we will always rise and return to the "better" us and recover our joy when our foundation is built on Christ.

Paul's main message in Philippians chapter four is to rejoice and to be cheerful and joyous in every season of life! Do not be anxious or worried about a thing; but instead, pray with faith-filled requests and overflowing gratitude. For Paul to advocate such a positive outlook is impressive when you consider where he was when he documented these thoughts. Paul was detained in the dingy dungeons of a Mamertine prison awaiting a sentence of death by decapitation.

This is usually not the time for someone to write a letter themed on rejoicing, but Paul would beg to differ. Even when life's circumstances would take a turn for the worse, Paul's perception and spiritual maturity would seem to be getting better. That is why we did not find him soaking in discouragement or wallowing in self-pity. He does not use his only line of communication to convey grievances about the conditions of his stay. With the absence of windows, light, and indoor plumbing, and having to sleep in proximity to stenches of urine and who knows what, you would think that Paul would have composed complaints to the readers of his letter. He could have penned: "This is a cruel, undeserved ending for someone who has spent years of dedicated service to the name of Jesus." On the contrary, he uses his energy and time to magnify God and the good news of Jesus Christ rather than exalt his problems. This is a prime example of what we can call an unshakeable foundation.

If you ever wanted a profound, clear understanding on how a foundation can make all the difference in our life, especially in storm seasons, we would turn to this scriptural teaching from Jesus:

> "Everyone who hears my teaching and applies it to his life can be compared to a wise man who built his house on an unshakable foundation.

When the rains fell and the flood came, with fierce winds beating upon his house, it stood firm because of its strong foundation. But everyone who hears my teaching and does not apply it to his life can be compared to a foolish man who built his house on sand. When it rained and rained and the flood came, with wind and waves beating upon his house, it collapsed and was swept away."

(Matthew 7:24-27 TPT)

You cannot stormproof your life, but you can certainly stormproof your foundation. Let me give you a working definition of a storm, according to Biblical terminology, before we continue onward.

A violent attempt to assault a fortified place by scaling the walls or forcing the gates to be breached.

A rushing, raging, violent agitation.

A disturbance to peace, priorities, and promise.

Affliction; calamity; distress; adversity.

So how do we build a foundation that will endure the waiting, outlast the storms; keep us focused, and fiercely strong? Well, Jesus did give us the answer in securing this foundation when He said, "Everyone who hears my teaching and applies it to his life can be compared to a wise man who built his house on an unshakable foundation" (Matthew 7:24 TPT).

IN THE WAITING

How to Build

According to Jesus, by hearing and obeying the Lord you are building a fortified ground that will cause you to stand and stay the course. How does that work? Does that mean that we become unsusceptible to the effects of a storm by simply following a bunch of Biblical standards? Is it just about obeying the Bible? I have witnessed many Christians "follow" the mandates of the book for years and then suddenly enter the drop-off zone caused by one furious wind from the storms of life. Going from a one-hundred, all-in pace, to zero and gone. They went from faithfully following Jesus, to forsaking their entire source of faith. We can follow rules, but rules without relationship is just dead religion.

Anytime we place obedience before relationship (the what before the why), we are building a hollow foundation that will soon enough fall into pieces after years of pacing on its fragile surface. Why we do things, the motive behind our movement, is what consecrates our relationship with the Lord. One of the scriptures I personally use to steer the purity of my motives as a believer is found in the gospel of Matthew.

> "Examine your motives to make sure you're not showing off when you do your good deeds, only to be admired by others; otherwise, you will lose the reward of your heavenly Father."
> (Matthew 6:1 TPT)

That teaching always smacks me in the face. To know that you can perform a good deed and still lose the reward of the Father is a revelation we cannot afford to ignore. It goes to show us that our motives, the very reason why we do things, is the key to reward, promise, and progression. In a similar fashion, relationship is the key to why we would obey the Lord.

For this relationship to be authentic, it must entail these two characteristics: trust and love. If these are not the motives to why we hear and obey, we deprive the strength needed for our foundation.

Trust and Love

"Trust in the Lord with all your heart
And do not lean on your own understanding."
(Proverbs 3:5 NASB)

I will not obey; at least from an affectionate place, something or someone I do not trust. On the other hand, I will obey and surrender to someone's leadership if I am convinced they are trustworthy.

It takes a lot less effort to trust someone when we know that they have our best interest in mind, or they have a history of walking in righteous integrity and faithfulness. I would especially trust in someone who loved me enough to willingly sacrifice their own life in order to take the fall for mine, even when I did not deserve to be off the hook. (Hint, hint). Jesus has adequately proven to us, beyond any doubt, that He is trustworthy. This is good news, because ultimately you are not trusting in a promise, but the person who made the promise. You would also need to trust that the person has the ability and power to bring the promise to fruition.

If I pronounced before you that I will be raising taxes in California, I am pretty sure you would not take that statement too seriously. Now if the Governor of the state broadcasted their intention to raise taxes, you can be sure it will be much more believable. Although the same statement was conveyed, we gain a greater level of trust of its fulfillment when the one who has the authority to make it happen speaks.

Are you ready to impartially trust in the person Jesus with all of your heart? The one and only Jesus, whom God has exalted and crowned King and Lord of all (see 1 Timothy 6:15 TPT)? You would be placing your life in the hands of the One who has the supreme authority and ability to take you from one realm of life to another. He will take you from ashes to beauty, rags to riches, pain to perfection. All you would need to do is trust His way and respect the process just as much as you respect the promise. When you're called to hear and obey divine instructions that might feel illogical in nature at times or seem statistically impossible, you must trust that He knows what He is doing. This is the relationship we are called into—a relationship of radical trust. Without it, our foundation is weakened—and we will not be able to stand when standing is required.

The next spiritual material that stabilizes our foundation is our love for the Lord. Jesus told His disciples:

> "Loving me empowers you to obey my commands."
> (John 14:15 TPT)

Love is the most powerful force that causes people to stay the course. We can literally measure the strength of our foundation by the intimacy we have with Jesus. When our heart burns for the Lord, we desperately long to walk in obedience to Him.

Once I allow my awestruck wonder and passion for the Lord to indistinctly dissipate and my heart affection to recede, then everything I'm called to do will suffer. How we love will determine how we live. Love must be the primary pursuit and the main motive anchored in our faith. According to Paul's revelation teaching in 1 Corinthians 13, when love is absent, our actions are recorded as empty and vain. Even in our spiritually inclined efforts, we might be doing good deeds—but without the right motives, we are not adding any strength to our foundation.

Take a moment to allow these scriptures that speak of us as lovers of God to solidify the standards in the core application of your life.

> "...the lives of his lovers are deeply rooted and firmly planted."
> (Proverbs 12:3 TPT)

> "...a life lived loving God bears lasting fruit..."
> (Proverbs 11:30 TPT)

> "Confidence and strength flood the hearts of the lovers of God who live in awe of him..."
> (Proverbs 14:26 TPT)

> "The lovers of God who chase after righteousness will find all their dreams come true: an abundant life drenched with favor and a fountain that overflows with satisfaction."
> (Proverbs 21:21 TPT)

> "The wicked are blown away by every stormy wind. But when a catastrophe comes, the lovers of God have a secure anchor."
> (Proverbs 10:25 TPT)

In order to gain depth and maturity, love must be nurtured. With that said, it is vital for us to contribute to the growth of our love for God by tending to it daily. It is similar to a marriage. For love to stay alive and thrive, the covenant must be renewed regularly. As far as I can remember, I have verbally expressed my devotion to my wife every day for the past twenty years. My goal is to make my devotion real and meaningful. I refuse to flippantly throw out an "I love you" with an obligated tone, and instead I make it a point to feel the emotions and capture in my thoughts, all the wonderful, unique things I adore and appreciate about her. In the same way, we can also cultivate the evolvement of our love for the Lord. Truthfully, the Lord is easy to love. We can find many things to love about Him. God is sincerely the most gracious, faithful, loving, kindest, forgiving, compassionate, and thoughtful being that exists. Get to know God as He truly is, and I guarantee you'll find Him irresistible.

The remarkable part of it all is His love for us. Though God knows every detail and every aspect of our life—including our flaws and weaknesses—the Bible says nothing can separate us from His love (see Romans 8:39 NLT). At the cross, He seemed to have found a thousand reasons to love us, and no reasons to reject us. It is because of love that you and I are saved and set free and have a destiny. His love is why He grooms us in the waiting. If you think about it, our love is really just a response to His love. Open your heart to Him and I guarantee that will open your heart for Him.

The Storm Validates Our Foundation

We learned that to have a storm-stopping, fortified foundation, we must do what Jesus revealed to us. We must hear His teaching and apply it to our lives (see Matthew 7:24 TPT). We also learned and must never forget, that hearing and obeying is the outcome of a personal, intimate relationship with the Lord—built on the purest form of trust and love.

With this foundation, life will move with momentum in the right direction even in turbulent times. We can continue to be tested and grow in character and conduct, because our roots in the Lord are keeping us firmly planted.

I love how Paul used the foundation he had in storms to validate his apostleship. In 2 Corinthians chapter eleven, a group of leaders, who were basically masquerading as apostles, began to publicly question Paul's apostolic position. To build a case for himself, Paul could have spoken about the supernatural miracles he experienced, from his handkerchief delivering people from demons (see Acts 19:12 TPT), to raising the dead (see Acts 20:10 TPT). He does not boast about these inexplicable encounters, but rather speaks of his trials to endorse his authenticity. Here was his list taken from 2 Corinthians 11:23-27 TPT:

1. Dragged into prisons.
2. Received countless beatings.
3. Flogged excessively, even to the point of death.
4. Five times he received thirty-nine lashes.
5. Three times he was beaten with rods.
6. Shipwrecked three times.
7. Survived dangerous situations including perilous rivers and robbers.
8. Toiled to the point of exhaustion, enduring cold and sleepless nights, and frequently deprived of food and water.

Paul listed his hardships instead of his miraculous moments in order to say that he had been through many storms, but he was still standing and running his race. In fact, he was just getting better instead of getting worse, despite the difficulties he had to overcome. The attitude that concludes Paul's point was: Let's see these people who are posing as "super-apostles" try and go through just one of my trials and then we will see who's the real apostle.

Paul was not interested in their accomplishments and influence, or how well they spoke when given a platform. He measured their authenticity by seeing what it would take to discourage them, and what it would take to cause them to quit. Paul was getting to the point of wanting to know how strong their foundation was in Christ.

What is the strength of your foundation? Can you identify what it would take to break down what you have internally built up in the Lord? We don't have to wait until something happens to find out, we can ask the Lord. Is there something in your foundation that must be torn down and rebuilt? Maybe there is something you need to add that is missing. At any rate, I beseech you to build, build, and build. So, like Paul, you will live a steadfast, immoveable life as you serve the mighty Kingdom of God.

8
Times of Testing

Every year on Christmas Eve, we traditionally indulge in steaks and a late-night movie with our good friends, Cory and Tera. Since this couple travels frequently as entertainers, we usually stay clear from exchanging gifts and just use this time to connect and enjoy each other's company. I knew this customary sequence would not last too long considering this couple is truly one of the most generous and compassionate human beings we know. It is in their nature to empower others, lift the downtrodden, and be a blessing when the opportunity arises. You can probably guess where I am going with this. On one of the occasions, they could not resist buying us gifts. I was handed a unique, novelty gift that at first glance I could not discern its function. It appeared to be some sort of large hook or cane with several golf-ball shaped knobs protruding out from the main stem of this gadget. I knew it was something special and thoughtful, so I gave my friends a beaming smile and expressed how thankful I was for such a wonderful gift. Eventually I was relieved from the mystery as Cory began to share how my "massage stick" works.

Have you ever received a gift and pretended to know what it was for? If so, you might not have acquired the full benefit of that gift. I know that if I was not given the proper guidance to the gift's purpose that my friends had given me, I would have utilized it for something other than what it was intended for. That usually becomes the case—when we do not know what something is for, we misuse it.

My wife's parents, who are from Brazil, came to stay with us in Los Angles for a few months. During their flight they were served a breakfast that is traditionally not on the menu in their household. It was pancakes! They are familiar with pancakes, as most are, but they just do not have much experience consuming what we consider a staple breakfast item. Every component was set before them to create a tasty morning meal—pancakes, butter, and in my eyes, the star of the show—syrup. Without speaking a lick of English, and not knowing the purpose for each piece presented, they dove in and took their best shot at enjoying an American classic. As a result, my in-laws had eaten the pancakes dry, without any spread or topping, and they had taken the container that held the syrup and drank it directly from the box as if they were taking an espresso shot. Again, when we do not know what something is for, we will often misuse it.

One Thing Leads to Another

Patience is a gift and must be "used" the right way to benefit us. If we do not steward well what God has given us, we pay the price for everything we could have been and everything we could have had.

In this scripture you'll see how things pertaining to the process are interconnected. Everything matters. Like an ecological system or like an infrastructure that is needed to operate a society or enterprise, one thing will always lead to another; so, if one step is left out the end-goal is never reached.

> "...Even in times of trouble we have a joyful confidence, knowing that our pressures will develop in us patient endurance. And patient endurance will refine our character, and proven character leads us back to hope."
>
> (Romans 5:3-4 TPT)

It is in times of trouble and through the pressures of life that patience has a chance to develop. Until patience is established, character cannot be acquired. Without character, we will not be led to hope. Without hope, we have no purposeful direction towards the future.

As an example, there are fundamental constants and quantities in the universe that are marked at the most impeccably precise position. If just one of these constants, such as the force of gravity or oxygen, were altered as slight as the width of a hair strand, there would be no physical life existing on planet Earth. By design, God has fine-tuned every physical law to cohesively work together. They were meant to work in perfect harmony. If one physical constant abruptly changes, it would not matter if the rest remained dialed to their exact placement. One would affect the other and we would be left with total annihilation of every living organism.

The same goes for patience, character, and hope. They must work together in succession in order to sustain the life of our destiny. One must succeed to assist the other. If not, the spiritual ecosystem is interrupted, and we are left stuck in the mud. The wheels are spinning but we are not moving very far.

There is much to say about each of these qualities; but in this chapter, I want to focus on character. In the Bible it says:

> "Those with good character walk on a smooth path, with no detour or deviation."
>
> (Proverbs 11:5 TPT)

Character

Character seems to keep the path before us less bumpy, with fewer obstacles and detours. That is to imply that when character is cultivated, we accelerate. We move out of the waiting at a faster pace.

From a Biblical standpoint, good character can be defined as the godly nature and virtues that are distinctive to an individual. As a caution, do not get character mixed up with what we call personality. The word personality comes from the word persona, which was originally used to describe an actor's role in ancient Greek theatrical plays. Today, personality is the side of us we want the world to see; the outward, social image we display to others. Character goes beyond that. It originates from a Greek verb that means to engrave. Character is the nature of the inner being that is engraved in our heart. It is who you are, not just in action, but also in motives. Many people can find a reason to do a moral act that everyone will visibly see, but that does not necessarily mean they have built within them godly character. The motive that is engraved in their heart is what measures the character. I like what some Christian leaders have said over the years: "Character is who you are when no one is looking."

When God prepares you for a promise, He will test your character. He does not test your anointing. He does not test your gift. He will test your character and do it over and over to gauge your readiness.

Tests are a part of life. To receive a promotion, to acquire a degree, to act in a play, or to drive a vehicle on the road, you must be tested. If the world knows the evolution to any forward movement requires testing, how much more should we know as citizens of Heaven? We represent a greater Kingdom and carry a greater responsibility. In preparation for a Kingdom mission, even Jesus—as perfect as He was—needed to be tested.

Jesus Needed the Wilderness

> "Afterward, the Holy Spirit led Jesus into the lonely wilderness in order to reveal his strength against the accuser by going through the ordeal of testing."
>
> (Matthew 4:1 TPT)

Jesus was led by God's Spirit to be tested and to confront the accuser outside of His normal environment, separated from family and friends. The test was to reveal His strength against the accuser, apart from any type of influence or dependency, other than trusting in God. (As a side note, I love that the main purpose of the test is to reveal our strength, not expose our weaknesses).

It was important for Jesus to experience the test upfront, before He was launched full-throttle into His mission. The test showed that He can handle any temptation the accuser could conjure up and it was the confidence Jesus needed for His assignment. In hindsight, the testing in the wilderness helped create this final outcome that is spoken of in Hebrews 4:15 NLT, "He faced all of the same testings we do, yet he did not sin."

Wherever the Holy Spirit leads us, His purpose will always be to prepare us for our destiny and to show us our strength, even if it feels like we're in a wilderness at the time.

In all honesty, it would be nice to be tested when we are at our best, but it does not seem to work that way when it pertains to Kingdom training. In the case of Jesus, the Bible says He was extremely weak and famished when He was under the test in the wilderness (see Matthew 4:2 TPT). I'm sure His human side would have preferred to be at His full strength mentally, physically, and spiritually, before facing the foe that wanted to devour Him. Nobody would want to show up physically ill, mentally overwhelmed with problems, and unprepared for the most important job interview of their career. Who would want to be tested in a physical obstacle challenge with a twisted ankle and a pounding headache? We all want to be at our very best when we are tested, but that request is not always fulfilled. In fact, it often seems like when we are down to our last few dollars, and our car is on the fritz, and the people closest to us are creating a mess, God says, "It is time to test your character." I am not complaining, but if Heaven had a suggestion box, the testing times might be something I would petition.

Joseph Needed Character

The test might not arrive at a moment that feels convenient, but I assure you its purpose is purely to promote you. As a testimony, the saga of Joseph in the book of Genesis reveals how someone can move from process to promise successfully through the growth of character.

At a young age, Joseph received a prophetically divine dream showing that he would possess some sort of authority to rule over others. At the time, Joseph was an arrogant, immature, boastful little daddy's boy that childishly hid behind the shield of his father. He would have ruled his inheritance with a prideful heart and a heavy hand, but God managed to utterly transform the disposition of Joseph.

> "Until the time came to fulfill his dreams, the Lord tested Joseph's character."
> (Psalm 105:19 NLT)

For about a decade and a half, through the entire run of his trials he was being trained and tested for the dream God had given him. Joseph endured loss and betrayal when he was separated from his family after his brothers heinously sold him into slavery to foreigners. He was then falsely accused of a sexual assault, which led him to prison, adding to the disappointments and misfortunes of his journey. Although it seemed like the dream was getting far away from Joseph, these adverse times had become the antidote needed to thrust forth the new, upright, compassionate, and godly Joseph that eventually ruled over the most powerful empire in the world. With a strong foundational character, he governed the entire Egyptian community and used his power to forgive his brothers and to rescue Israel and the world from the tragedies of a severe famine.

Joseph impacted history not because of a prophecy over his life, not because of the spiritual gifts he was given, but because of the character that was developed within him. You can have all the power in the world, but if you do not have character, that power will actually work against you. In the waiting, our character must be tested, or the promise will hurt us more than helps us.

> "In the same way that gold and silver are refined by fire, the Lord purifies your heart by the tests and trials of life."
>
> (Proverbs 17:3 TPT)

A New Reality for Jesus

Another reason why Jesus needed to be tested in the wilderness was to prepare Him for what He had not yet experienced—persecution. It is safe to assume Jesus was a very likable, kind, and humble kid in His community. The Bible says Jesus was an obedient child to His parents and He had been given continual favor with mankind before He made His assignment known publicly (see Luke 2:51-52 NKJV). That being said, before the wilderness, Jesus had not yet suffered aggressive assaults of hostility and persecution. He had not yet experienced an angry mob drag Him to an edge of a cliff, ready to hurl Him off (see Luke 4:29 TPT). Jesus did not yet know what it was like to have constant hatred and harassment from the population and the heads of society, who also conspired to kill Him (see John 11:53 TPT).

His entire human experience was about to radically change, therefore Jesus had to be tested and ready to respond to anything that might occur in the path to the promises. Thankfully, before Jesus faced His first persecution-level conflict, He had already prepared for the battles by setting standards that would become key foundations in His life. You will find these life-decrees within the three responses to the three temptations in the wilderness:

1. True life is found in every word that proceeds from the mouth of God.
2. Never put the Lord God to a test.
3. Worship Him only.

Jesus was ready for a new reality because He cultivated these convictions that became pillars in times of persecution. He believed our life should be governed by every word that God speaks, that we should never test God but rather trust God, and that our greatest affections and worth should be ascribed to God. This is why we find the same Jesus in trials and triumphs. This was the character that was engraved in our Messiah.

Forty

The wilderness that Jesus experienced can represent the waiting for a believer. I am not suggesting that our waiting seasons will not exceed forty days, but that His wilderness battle can stand as a model for our lives because the number forty prophetically symbolizes two things: time periods for transitions and testing for the sake of spiritual advancement. We can see this by these examples:

> Moses lived in the luxuries of Egypt for *forty* years and then the desert for an additional *forty* years, as intervals to prepare his destiny to deliver Israel.

> A new covenant and way of life was formed as Moses spent *forty* days with God on Mount Sinai to receive the commandment tablets.

> The testing for the promised land promotion occurred for *forty* years among the Israelites as seen in Deuteronomy 8:2 NLT: "…the Lord your God led you through the wilderness for these forty years, humbling you and testing you to prove your character, and to find out whether or not you would obey his commands."

> When Moses felt it was time to make their move into the promise, he sent Hebrew spies to survey the land for *forty* days.

> To begin a new era with Noah and his family, it rained for *forty* days and flooded the earth.

For the city of Nineveh to be saved from destruction, Jonah gave them *forty* days to humble themselves, repent, and change their ways.

After the resurrection, Jesus spent *forty* days teaching His followers about the Kingdom of God to ignite their hearts to invade the Earth with the new covenant.

The number forty was the prophetic language for several waiting periods with the end goal of transitioning into something new. This is why we can regard the testing that Jesus experienced in the wilderness as something to provide insight for our personal time of testing in the waiting.

As perceived earlier, we gained standards of Jesus by His response to each temptation. Now with a greater, prophetic understanding to the relevance of that encounter, I would like to share one of the three temptations so we can be aware and ready for the deceiver's trickery in the waiting.

Temptations

In the wilderness, the enemy took three shots at Jesus—three temptations—that were intended to overturn the Messiah's mission. Each premeditated attempt was a strategy formulated by years of contemplating human behavior. This is why the father of lies offered Jesus the same temptations people repeatedly give into.

The temptation I want to examine in this chapter was the first temptation towards Jesus. I believe this is one of the main tests that we tackle in the waiting.

> "And after fasting for forty days, Jesus was extremely weak and famished. Then the tempter

came to entice him to provide food by doing a miracle. So he said to Jesus, "How can you possibly be the Son of God and go hungry? Just order these stones to be turned into loaves of bread.""

(Matthew 4:2-3 TPT)

Knowing that Jesus was extremely weak and famished, the tempter offered Him food. At a glance, that doesn't seem too much of a threat to the call of Jesus. Isn't he the devil, shouldn't he offer something evil and destructive such as hallucinate drugs or chaotic behavior? What is with the temptation to eat a piece of delicious bread?

What we need to recognize is that the enemy did not tempt Jesus with food, he tempted Jesus with desire. He figured if Jesus had not eaten in forty days and He is famished, His greatest physical desire must be food. The enemy was banking on desire—because without it, temptation does not exist.

"Let no one say when he is tempted, "I am tempted by God"; for God cannot be tempted by evil, nor does He Himself tempt anyone. But each one is tempted when he is drawn away by his own desires and enticed."

(James 1:13-14 NKJV)

If you absolutely despise the taste of chocolate, and I offer you a lifetime supply of Godiva's finest candy bars at the lowest possible price on the market, you would not be wrestling with any sort of temptation. There is no level of temptation, because there is no desire.

In fact, every proposition of the tempter is positively powerless and will not succeed, unless you desire and are enticed by what is being presented to you. If you are a woman and deep down you desire self-affirmation because that was absent in the household that raised you, then trust me: the enemy will take that "need" and tempt you with the wrong man to fulfill that desire. If you were taught that success is based on your financial status and position in the business world, that would be a desire that the enemy could use to create opportunities that distort and twist your priorities.

Desire is to strongly long for, crave, or want something that you believe you must have in order to bring you satisfaction. The enemy knows that wherever your desire is directed, that is where you will be the most vulnerable. Not only does he propose temptations that feed your unchecked desires, but he will also create desires that you did not have before. Eve did not have a desire to violate the boundaries of God's command to not eat from the tree of the knowledge of good and evil (see Genesis 2:17 NKJV). What was not a desire before, become one through the deception of the tempter.

> "So when the woman saw that the tree was good for food, that it was pleasant to the eyes, and a tree desirable to make one wise, she took of its fruit and ate."
> (Genesis 3:6 NKJV)

In the fall of man, the enemy had to create a desire first in order for there to be a temptation. By opening her eyes to the enemy's suggestion and allowing her curiosity to be aroused, the tree suddenly became desirable. Eve went from having no interest, complying and quoting God's strict orders and consequences, to feeling an irresistible urge for the forbidden fruit. That is the power of desire that the enemy depends on to take us down.

Here is something to be considered—what if our utmost desire in life was to bring pleasure to the heart of the Lord? Like

Paul who said, "My supreme passion is to please God" (Galatians 1:10 TPT). If my greatest yearning and desire is to love, follow, and obey Jesus, that desire will lead me to only be tempted by what Jesus offers me.

You might think, especially during the "honeymoon" stage of becoming a Christian, that nothing can interfere with your new-found faith and relationship with the Savior. Then you reach a transitional waiting period in your life where God appears to be quiet and the old, ungodly desires are blaring for attention. At this time, that deeply rooted desire for Jesus alone can come in to play and unarm every compromising lure the enemy tries to attract you with.

Never forget, you can only be tempted by what you desire. Therefore, be open to your desires being examined, assessed, and evaluated in the waiting; because our heart cannot be trusted until it is tested.

The Test Will Authenticate

We would not place our life in the hands of a surgeon who has not been properly trained. It does not matter if the surgeon's sweet, eighty-year-old grandmother says he or she is the best there is in the medical field. My assurance must come from a reputable university that has tested and approved the surgeon's ability before I trust him or her to cut open my body. Likewise, it should only be the "university" of the Kingdom of God that endorses and decides if we are ready for the next opportunity that is on our destiny-path. Be patient, let the testing take its course, and if you miss something, learn and re-take the test. God knows when to graduate you from one stage of life to another. Trust Him, because if you arrive somewhere without the acceptable preparation and process, you will be crushed by the weight of the blessing and spiritual responsibility.

> "An inheritance gained hurriedly at the beginning
> Will not be blessed in the end."
> (Proverbs 20:21 NASB)

> "If your faith remains strong, even while surrounded by life's difficulties, you will continue to experience the untold blessings of God! True happiness comes as you pass the test with faith, and receive the victorious crown of life promised to every lover of God!"
> (James 1:12 TPT)

9

Finding Freedom

I love watching hilarious animal scenarios that are caught on tape, especially when the stronger, more powerful creature is intimidated and backed down by the weaker one. When a lovable, tiny kitten fearlessly chases away a big and brawny pit bull, we can definitely chalk that up as a comical moment. On the other hand, it is less amusing when the superior being is dominated by the inferior being in the spiritual realm.

The Bible clearly states, "He who is in you is greater than he (Satan) who is in the world" (1 John 4:4 AMP). Even though this is true, we commonly find Christians live as though they are no match to the diabolical force sent to trouble them. As long as this facade stands, the smaller will always defeat the greater.

A good segment of our time spent in the waiting is used to discover the magnitude of our spiritual grandeur. The Word of God tells us that we are able to do exceedingly abundantly above all that we ask or think, according to the power that works in us (see Ephesians 3:20 NKJV). Did you get that? It says, "according to the power that works in us." When we became born again, the Spirit of God—the same Spirit that raised Jesus from the dead—and His power, came to live and dwell in us. Prior to that wonderful day, spiritually speaking, we were subdued by darkness (see Ephesians 5:8 NKJV), lost in our trespasses (see Ephesians 2:1 NKJV), deceived and enslaved to the powers of this world (see Titus 3:3 NKJV). Now we have become a new creation that can do all things through the explosive strength of Christ that is infused in us (see 2 Corinthians 5:17, Philippians 4:13 TPT).

If this is the reality believers are graced with, why do so many of us inhabit lowly, broken, and defeated lives for years on end? How do believers end up treading below their potential, limiting their possible prospective, and oppressing their divine power within? This should not be the case for any follower of Jesus. We all have the ability to rise above any situation since we have the greater one residing in us.

Slaves to the Inferior

The best way to uncover this paradox is by analyzing Israel's inception to slavery. The words "more and mightier" in the passage we will review describe the superior position Israel had over Egypt. Israel's population had dominated the Egyptian natives, making their nation stronger, mightier, and more powerful than Egypt could ever be on their best day. Yet, the startling outcome that baffles the mind of us all is that Egypt ruled and enslaved Israel for a whopping four hundred and thirty years. How did Egypt possibly pull that off? Let's take a look.

> "Now there arose a new king over Egypt…And he said to his people, "Look, the people of the children of Israel are MORE and MIGHTIER than we; come, let us deal shrewdly with them, lest they multiply, and it happen, in the event of war, that they also join our enemies and fight against us, and so go up out of the land." Therefore they

set taskmasters over them to afflict them with their BURDENS…But the more they afflicted them, the more they multiplied and grew. And they were in dread of the children of Israel. So the Egyptians made the children of Israel serve with rigor. And they made their lives BITTER with hard BONDAGE…"

(Exodus 1:8-14 NKJV, emphasis added)

Egypt was in a panic! They were anxiously alarmed by the frightening fact that Israel had the ability to conquer and control their prestigious empire. With that threat overshadowing their monarchy, the king of Egypt devised a plan that has worked throughout the human race, and that is: if you are able to oppress the people, you will be able to control the people.

We become what we believe about ourselves. There are thousands of stories, (some that I know personally) where a spouse or some sort of authority figure has mentally oppressed someone to the point where that someone lived their life subordinate to those false beliefs. I've also witnessed people who have walked away from those abusive situations, only to end up in a positive, empowering environment that led them to discover what they were not able to do under the bondage of lies. Some of these people were women who were told constantly that they are idiotic and incapable of accomplishing much, only to later find the truth that they can do anything through Jesus Christ. Consequently, these women have become radiant daughters, loving mothers, community leaders, successful entrepreneurs, revivalists, and mighty ministers that are impacting countless lives.

If only the Israelites recognized that they were mightier before the king's plan was set in motion. Then the plot that consisted of the following three tactical acts that was shown in the passage we read, would not have coerced the fall of Israel.

1. They afflict them with BURDENS.
2. They made their lives BITTER.
3. They place upon them heavy BONDAGES.

Oppression

The enemy is not getting any bigger, but we are getting smaller if we do not forbid this pattern to overtake us. Any time we are weighed down with *burdens,* harboring *bitterness,* and stifled by mental *bondages,* oppression is certain and the best of us will not rise—but instead be restrained.

Since burdens, bitterness, and bondages have solely become the reason why an inferior people group ruled Israel, we must learn how to be free from these things. We can turn to God in this area because it is His perfect pleasure to empower His children. According to the narrative in Acts 10:38 NKJV, Jesus was commissioned to exert the power of the Holy Spirit to do good and to heal all who were oppressed by the devil. Jesus did not come to Earth strictly to forgive your sins, but also to free you from every demonically inspired oppression that prohibits the power and purpose on your life to flourish.

Oppression always tries to hypnotically fasten itself to us wherever we go. Even when years have passed and we are far from the person or place that originally instigated oppressiveness, we may still retract to the responses of that oppressed mindset. The Israelites experienced the same drawback. Though they escaped from the hands of their Egyptian taskmasters, their journey to the promised land revealed that their identity was still confined to a slave's mentality.

Maybe this is all too familiar for you. You might be a victim of having past experiences regulate your future course and letting temporary moments leave a permanent mark. You do not need to hold on to any unpleasant memory from the past. You can be loosed and liberated. You can be free from a life held back by burdens, bitterness, and bondage; for it is our God, in the waiting, that surgically undoes the damages of an oppressed life.

Burden

When you theologically dig for a Biblical term for burdens, here is what you might find:

That which is grievous, wearisome, and oppressive.

To lay on a heavy load.

To encumber with weight.

If I ran the distance of a mile, I would likely be a bit winded, break a slight sweat, and be in serious need of hydration. Even though it was a physical challenge, I would be able to accomplish the goal and enjoy the value of that workout. In contrast, what would happen if I ran the same footpath, but now with fifty pounds of weight strapped on my back? The extra, overwhelming heap would turn what would have been a pleasant, endurable run into a stressful, tiring task to complete. As a matter of fact, by consciously knowing weight has been added to me, I would lack the inspiration to even attempt the run—causing me to quit before I begin. I mean, why even try? Who can bear such a load?

Burdens are the load we carry in life. The nagging cares, worries, fears, imaginations, and present troubles are all a part of the burdensome build up. If we are not watchful, the weight can feel like we are under an unbearable nuisance that is too much for one to handle. We might not be able to deal with such a strain, but the Lord is able. Psalm 55:22 NKJV declares that if we permit God to manage the burdens of our life, then we become supernaturally sustained under His care. This is good news because the calling of our life does come with challenges and we need God's divine, burden-removing relief lest we find ourselves circling dry land as the Israelites did for way too long.

Lighter

There are several scriptures that summon us to live "lighter," such as Hebrews 12:1 NLT that cautions us to strip off every weight that slows us down or we will not be able to run with endurance the race God has set before us. There are other similar themes that direct our hearts to not worry or fear (see Matthew 6:25, Isaiah 41:10 NASB), but the one I delight in the most is:

> "Then Jesus said, "Come to me, all of you who are weary and carry heavy burdens, and I will give you rest. Take my yoke upon you. Let me teach you, because I am humble and gentle at heart, and you will find rest for your souls. For my yoke is easy to bear, and the burden I give you is light.""
> (Matthew 11:28-30 NLT)

If you were to take a spiritual leader's "yoke," especially in the days of Jesus, you would be agreeing and adhering to that Rabbi's interpretation and application of the holy scriptures. You would be completely committed to imitate their ministry model and carry the weight and demand of their ways. So in essence, Jesus invited all who carried heavy burdens to simply unload, because living from His view of the world was light and easy compared to any other way.

We fall into a perfect peace and rest for our souls when we live by the yoke of the Kingdom. Anything less than a Christ-centered faith, love, and grace can add unnecessary weight to our life. The Apostle John, who had surrendered his entire life devoted to the yoke of Jesus, assures us in this passage that: "his commands don't weigh us down as heavy burdens" *(*1 John 5:3 TPT). The commands of Jesus are not burdensome, but the way we interpret His commands can be. If we filter each thing that the Lord is asking of us through our brokenness, our greatest worries, or our shame-filled experiences, then the commands become an added stress to our life. The Lord's commands are there to empower us, not bury us. They just need to be translated through the right lens, or else light and easy will become heavy and hard.

I remember listening to a sermon where the preacher spoke about his encounter with a pastoral leader who had been in charge of four thousand churches in Africa. The preacher was astounded by how one man can handle the "burden" of overseeing so many churches that he asked, "How do you deal with the stress from the typical problems that take place in these church communities?" The man replied, "Problems? What problems?" He went on to say, "Whatever you look at gets bigger, so I look at Jesus, not the problems." His perception made managing four thousand churches light and easy and not a massive burden. In the waiting, we either have our eyes on problems or promises; and one of them is gaining weight.

Rules

Christians that have been subject to environments of religiosity (rules without relationship), usually run from "rules," being convinced that by excluding them, they will experience a "lighter" life. The truth is, fewer rules do not make us free; but rather, understanding the purpose of the rules gives us freedom. If a parent wanted their child to experience more freedom, I doubt their solution would be to take away all the rules and let them do whatever they want. That would actually be foolish because they would be jeopardizing the safety of their child. For their child to feel real freedom, the best thing to do is to help them fully grasp the reasons behind the rules—behind the "do not touch the hot stove." If they miss the purpose, they will mistakenly judge the parent as one who is irrationally strict, when they are actually thoughtful guardians who created protective boundaries to push them forward.

The bottom line is, we will not be able to reach our very best and run the full course of our race, unless we alleviate the weight of burdens. When we learn to completely surrender our cares to the Lord—whose ways are light and easy—and when we keep our eyes locked on the promise-keeper, Jesus, our burdens will start to lift. As we renew our relationship with the "rules," and realize that His commands are designed for our freedom and not to restrict our growth, problems will not become bigger than the Kingdom.

Bitter

The next area that has the ability to oppress our eminence is bitterness.

> "...make sure no one lives with a root of bitterness sprouting within them which will only cause trouble and poison the hearts of many."
> (Hebrews 12:15 TPT)

Bitterness is a vexing spiritual cancer that has invaded so many people's lives in the body of Christ. It can turn anything that is remotely good, into something bad. My wife likes to tease me about my dysfunctional taste palate. I could be eating something that is blatantly sweet, and I'll swear that I am tasting something sour. The one taste that I can identify clearly because of the way it overwhelms the taste buds is bitterness. You can add a tiny dash of a bitter substance to a liquid and the entire drink will pungently transform. Just like the scripture says, a little lie can permeate our entire belief system (see Galatians 5:9 TPT). Bitterness saturates our entire world. We can easily get consumed with the bitter failures of our past, the envy we have of others, shameful regrets, hurts we hold on to, grudges, resentment, jealousies, disappointments, offenses, and the list goes on and on.

Every negative experience can infect us, where we simply can no longer taste and see that the Lord is good as Psalm 34:8 NKJV directs us to, because all we taste is a heart filled with bitterness. Another passage puts it this way:

> "Is it possible that fresh and bitter water can flow out of the same spring? So neither can a bitter spring produce fresh water."
>
> (James 3:12 TPT)

Refreshing springs of God's living Word cannot share the same channel with bitter waters without being defiled. Bitterness has to be flushed out of our hearts.

Above All

I found out years ago that whatever clings to your heart controls your life. Since that revelation, the following scripture has been my anchor in anything I do.

> "Guard your heart above all else, for it determines the course of your life."
>
> (Proverbs 4:23 NLT)

To protect what we consider valuable, we will build fortified walls and gates, set up alarm and surveillance systems, and employ trained professionals to guard our goods. The more valuable the object, the more money is spent to preserve it. This is why the Lord says, above all else guard your heart. We are required to pay whatever the cost may be to defend the welfare of our innermost being, for it determines the course of our life.

Springs and wells in these ancient times had to be guarded diligently with extreme caution, because if any sort of contamination entered the water supply, it spoiled everything that was good and useful from that life source. Likewise, if bitterness nestles its way into the deep wells of our heart, even the good attributes of our life will suffer.

A Bitter-Free Plan

Being bitter is not rational. It never provides the power to change the situation nor does it make you feel any better; it always makes things worse. I do not think anyone really plans to be this way; but the problem is, they also do not plan *not* to be. For instance, I have met and partnered with many gifted Christians, anointed by the Lord, who have crashed in their calling due to a heart that became and remained bitter. This was not their intention, but because they did not have a working strategy on how *not* to become bitter, their hearts were left unguarded.

Bitterness can be provoked by envy or jealousy, or when things are not turning out the way we wish they would; but a common thread I have disclosed is that bitterness predominantly comes from a heart that has been hurt, and cannot seem to let go of that hurt.

As long as we keep focusing on what has been done to us and the injustice that we suffered, like a magnet we will be pulled back to that hurt—causing bitterness to sink deeper into the core consciousness of our heart. I know the trap all too well. We replay the situation in our mind, and each time we add a new, valid reason (often imagined) to keep our grudge fresh and flourishing. We keep feeding the "beast" by repeating the story to others, the story that assures our innocence and justifies our legit right to stay angry. This is why I believe that one of the major snares that keeps bitterness alive and its poison active is our lack of forgiveness.

With our entire eternal inheritance and spiritual freedom built on forgiveness, you would think it would be our specialty. That is often not the case in the church and we can seriously struggle in this area that we should actually be mastering. This is why forgiveness must start with a choice.

Years ago, I experienced the heartbreak of betrayal from a long-time friend and ministry partner. This caused a world of bitter feelings where I could not even hear this person's name without unkind sentiments seizing space in my heart. That is exactly when I knew I had to do whatever it took to extract every ounce of bitterness or it would cost me. I made a willing choice to walk the path of forgiveness even though my mind and emotions did not want to cooperate with that decision.

Forgiveness can be tricky. We can be convinced that forgiveness was settled once we uttered the words, "I forgive so-and-so" and attempt to control our negative thoughts and comments towards that person. That is a gallant start, and it should be commended. I certainly want to celebrate every type of effort that is made, but I must say; in the Kingdom, forgiveness goes much further. Our target must always be to forgive as Christ forgave us.

> "...forgiving one another in the SAME WAY you have been graciously forgiven by Jesus Christ. If you find fault with someone, release this SAME GIFT of forgiveness to them."
>
> (Colossians 3:13 TPT, emphasis added)

There is no other model of forgiveness that we should follow other than the way Jesus has forgiven us. When Jesus released us from our trespasses through our repentance, our sins were not only forgiven but also forgotten. According to the law of grace, Jesus was no longer permitted to hold them against us, because our offenses had been settled in the courts of Heaven through the cross of Christ. (See Jeremiah 31:34, Ephesians 1:7, Hebrews 8:12; 10:17-18 NASB).

When we choose to forgive as we have been forgiven, we are choosing to release all of our rights to hold the person's offense against them. That doesn't always mean your relationship will be reconciled to the same status you had before, because there could be issues that do not allow the friendship to bridge itself back together. You are simply stating that the person does not owe you anything, they do not need to earn your forgiveness, and that you are offering it as a gift, despite if it's received or rejected.

Now the gritty reality that often stumps the average Christian is that in order to truly forgive the same way Christ forgave, and to liberate us from every sense of bitterness, we must strive to furnish our heart with sincere love and well wishes for the one who stood against us as an enemy. It is one thing to say, "I will negate all bad thoughts towards my offender," but it is an entirely different thing to foster good thoughts for him or her. It is not that we are rewarding bad behavior, but instead we are reflecting the marvelous grace we freely received from a loving Father.

Jesus not only suffered to forgive us for our sins, but He also cheers for us. When we were defiantly offensive towards the ways of God, giving the Lord no good reason to wipe our slate clean, Jesus was not wishing evil upon us, but campaigning for our destiny and breakthrough. He wants the best for us even when we are behaving at our worst. This is the only standard for forgiveness for those who represent the Kingdom.

In my journey of Christ-like forgiveness, it took me close to a year to feel an earnest, heartfelt love and desire for good towards the one who betrayed me. During that time, I discovered that forgiveness is more about our relationship with God than the offender.

Bitterness will dissolve with a life devoted to forgiveness. If you can follow this scriptural layout for your life, your heart will be guarded from bitterness.

> "But if you will listen, I say to you, love your enemies and do something wonderful for them in return for their hatred. When someone curses you, bless that person in return. When you are mistreated and harassed by others, accept it as your mission to pray for them. To those who despise you, continue to serve them and minister to them…However you wish to be treated by others is how you should treat everyone else."
> (Luke 6:27-29,31 TPT)

Bondage

Bondages are the final scheme on our list that kept little Egypt in power over big Israel for many generations—and can keep us oppressed under the power of an inferior spirit during our lifetime. If we are in bondage, it means we are bound; and anytime something binds us, we are limited from functioning at our full divine capacity.

The Bible says that the truth sets us free (see John 8:32 NLT), which means the only thing that can keep us bound is a lie. Romans 6:16 TPT says you are bound to the one you choose to obey. If our heart believes and obeys any demonically-inspired lie or accusation, we have relinquished control in that area to the one who created the lie. We are detained in bondage until truth begins to break those chains.

To any lie that plagues your perception, there is a truth that can release you from that prison. Whether it is an assault against your adequacy or self-worth, you can build a wall of truth to guard your heart from these deceptions. It does not matter that I've been a Christian for twenty-two years and a pastor for twelve, I am just as vulnerable to lies as anyone else if truth is not before my eyes every day. I suggest you do the same, because the bottom line is—truth sets us free and lies keep us in bondage. If Israel would have known the truth, not only would they have remained free from Egypt's tyranny, but they could have actually reigned over them.

Taking Down Egypt

An ultimate price was paid for us to reign in this life. It is our inheritance to walk in Kingdom power and dominion over demonic entities and earthly obstacles. It would be an epic miss if you did not dismantle the influence of "Egypt" in your life while in the waiting. Commit to never let the oppression of burdens, bitterness, and bondages of the weaker spirit to cheat you out of everything you can be. I love you and pray this chapter has awakened the warrior within as I remind you once again that "the One who is living in you is far greater than the one who is in the world" (1 John 4:4 TPT).

10
Only God Can

My wife and I were called to the office of a pastor in a very peculiar way. It began with a phone call from our pastor in May of 2005, and he shared how he had carefully watched over us the last four years because, at that time, the Lord had shown him that we ought to be appointed to a pastoral position. I remember being so perplexed by the conversation, simply because becoming a pastor was not on our radar. It was the furthest thing from our mind as there has never been a discussion with my pastor or among us regarding this role in the church.

After hanging up the phone and reporting the news to my wife, the confusion that was whirling in my mind had only increased. We began to assume I must have misheard the details of the dialogue, because the typical order in the culture of that church was that you become ordained as an elder or have a high-ranking leadership position first before a pastoral position is offered. Aury and I were convinced that I had gotten my wires twisted and it was likely that we will be established as elders in the church. I know it seems silly that we did not just call my pastor to clarify what was muddled in our mind, but we prayed about it and declared to the Lord that whatever position we are given, we will serve in it faithfully. The very next month, in June of 2005, our pastor brought us to the stage and announced before the congregation, "Today we are ordaining Tymme and Aury Reitz as pastors." Glancing towards me and firmly squeezing my hand, my wife whispered, "I guess he did say pastor on the phone after all."

It can be presumed that in every waiting period, God is preparing us for something we do not even know about. We might vaguely know what future resolution we are sowing towards, training for, or even what spiritual test is opening the door to elevate us. But God, the author and finisher of our faith, does know (see Hebrews 12:2 NKJV).

David thought he was just protecting sheep by shielding them from lions and bears (see 1 Samuel 17:34-37 NKJV), but he had no clue that by simply doing his daily task with passion and persistence, he was actually being prepared to battle the giant, Goliath—a battle that would lead him to his prophetic destiny, the throne of Israel. In a similar way, Aury and I were blind to the fact that God was grooming us to be senior leaders and pioneers of a church. We were just simply surrendered to serving His Kingdom during those years that my pastor was examining our character and faith for this position.

By this example and by the scriptures I will share in this chapter, I firmly believe that the great God-promotions in our life will come when we have abandoned ourselves to the process by trusting the Lord's timing and how things will manifest. This point is beautifully expressed in the following passage:

> "This I know: the favor that brings promotion and power doesn't come from anywhere on earth, for no one exalts a person but God, the true judge of all…"
>
> (Psalm 75:6-7 TPT)

The truth is, earthly promotions can be produced without the intervention of God. It can be accomplished by human ingenuity and determination. But our divine purpose, the very things we were born to do while occupying the earth, can only be granted by God. To wait on the Lord is to wait for Him alone to exalt us to these positions at the perfect time (the time He perceives that we are ready). Depending on anyone other than God will always work against us.

> "This is what the Lord says: "Cursed are those who put their trust in mere humans, who rely on human strength...But blessed are those who trust in the Lord and have made the Lord their hope and confidence.""
>
> (Jeremiah 17:5,7 NLT)

Pressure to Promote Self

In this passage, cursed is the person because an obstacle is set between them and the Lord's blessing—something we cannot afford to block. Think about it: The primary things that the Lord has for us can be denied if our trust that pertains to our destiny is directed towards a human's ability to promote us.

Nobody but God should be trusted to carry you to your destiny, because nobody but God can. That was another thing that we can see shine in the life of David. He was a man who refused to manipulate and force an outcome outside of God's timing. He'd rather wait than receive the blessing prematurely.

You might remember, sometime after the Goliath takedown, Saul, the current king of Israel, was hunting David. Saul was jealous of all the fanfare David received from his big battle and wanted to end David's popularity by snuffing him out. In the course of the chase, David had the chance to permanently remove Saul from his position—the very position David was promised prophetically through the great prophet Samuel (see 1 Samuel 16:13 NKJV).

In the story that takes place in 1 Samuel chapter twenty-four, David had Saul cornered in a vulnerable position, and all he had to do is "pull the trigger" and seemingly his problems would have disappeared. In an instant, David could have traded the life of a fugitive—who was forced to hide in the recess of caves—for a life that anyone in their right mind coveted, the highest position of honor and authority in all of the land. For us, that would be like moving from a low-income shelter to the president's chair. It's a no-brainer to figure out which is better, the castle or the cave.

To pass up such an extravagant promotion was tough, especially since Saul was a corrupt, unreliable leader, and David loved his nation and knew that was not God's best for them. In addition to these facts, David's comrades—the six-hundred faithful soldiers who followed him—egged David on with this word "from the Lord":

> "Then the men of David said to him, "This is the day of which the Lord said to you, 'Behold, I will deliver your enemy into your hand, that you may do to him as it seems good to you.' ""
>
> (1 Samuel 24:4 NKJV)

They were all subliminally chanting, "Do it David! Do it! Do it!" To everyone around him, it made perfect sense. This was David's moment to embrace his destiny. He did not need to spend another day living this messy, stressful life. He could have freely (and some would say deservingly) indulged in the finest delicacies, riches, and comforts that would come from his prophetic inheritance as king. Additionally, as a major incentive, he would be permitted to marry the princess that was promised to him for defeating Goliath. Who could walk away from this favorable window of opportunity? Well, David did.

David knew that he was promised the throne and he also knew that Saul was the only one standing in the way of it. Most importantly, David knew that if God had made the promise, God will keep the promise, which meant it was not his job to remove Saul, but God's. So he spared the life of Saul, choosing to wait patiently for God to exalt him on His terms and timing.

Whatever we gain by our own effort, we must sustain by our own effort. If you started it, you have to finish it. God is not obligated to help you build something you created apart from Him, which you never want to do because anything you profit without God will eventually be measured as a loss.

Creating Isaacs or Ishmaels

The Lord had made a covenant promise with Abraham—a promise to give him a son that would be the seed to the rise of a nation set apart for His glory. After many years of trying to conceive along with being past the years of child-bearing, Abraham's wife, Sarah, proposed a plan that would get some wind behind the sails of this promise and help it move forward. As a solution, she suggested that Abraham impregnate Hagar, her household servant (or slave). The overall thought that was blueprinted in Sarah's mind was to use Hagar's son, who was named Ishmael, to "assist" God in His covenant. The well-meaning plan did not succeed, not for the lack of desiring God's promise to prevail, but because it was not done God's way. My belief is that Sarah's lack of patience is what caused the fourteen-year delay for Isaac to be born—the son that would fulfill the promise.

For us to comprehend what took place spiritually in this story, we can read Paul's revelation from this passage.

> "The Scriptures say that Abraham had two sons, one from his slave wife and one from his freeborn wife. The son of the slave wife was born in a human attempt to bring about the fulfillment of God's promise. But the son of the freeborn wife was born as God's own fulfillment of his promise."
>
> (Galatians 4:22-23 NLT)

What we do towards every vision we carry is either birthing Ishmaels or Isaacs. When we consent to cutting corners and compromising or try to coerce the God-given dream on our own, we create Ishmaels. And Ishmaels will never securely inherit the entire promise of God.

One of my motives for writing this book came from noticing those who share their grand vision from God with me. They will often express that waiting is the hardest part of it all. Many Christians will fall because of the waiting, while those who waited have everything God promised. Patience is always the key and Abraham eventually surrendered to that process (see Hebrews 6:15 TPT).

Exalts the Humble

In my journey to finish this race well, I have studied to learn from Old Testament figures who have started in their destiny strong only to end up crashing hard and losing everything. In observance of every individual that regressed, I can attest to a specific act relating to their ruin. The one characteristic that each person shared as the main reason for their downfall was pride. By a Biblical definition, what constitutes a person who is sinfully prideful is when ultimate confidence shifts from God to self.

The common denominator for every single fall and every single unfulfilled call in the Bible is mankind choosing their way over God's way. Pride can be our greatest enemy because the Word of God distinctly states that God opposes any of His people who are proud (see James 4:6, 1 Peter 5:5 NASB). If you think the devil is a difficult opponent, imagine what it is like with the almighty Creator standing in your way.

God is unable to promote someone to their purpose who is overrun with pride. On the contrary, when our lives reflect the beautiful humility of Jesus, we can expect to be exalted in every due season of our faith walk. In fact, according to these passages, there is no other way to be spiritually elevated than through humility.

> "...those who humble themselves will be EXALTED."
> (Luke 14:11 NLT, emphasis added)

> "Humble yourselves in the presence of the Lord, and He will EXALT YOU."
> (James 4:10 NASB, emphasis added)

> "If you bow low in God's awesome presence, he will eventually EXALT YOU as you leave the timing in his hands."
> (1 Peter 5:6 TPT, emphasis added)

Jesus, the co-creator of all that exists (see John 1:3 NLT), sacrificed His life for all of humanity. We witnessed the single greatest act of humility, which was followed with the greatest exaltation that could be given. Could it be that the greater the humility, the greater the promotion?

> "Being found in appearance as a man, He humbled Himself by becoming obedient to the point of death, even death on a cross. FOR THIS REASON also, God HIGHLY EXALTED Him, and bestowed on Him the name which is above every name."
> (Philippians 2:8-9 NASB, emphasis added)

Blame and Entitlement

Jesus could not have been promoted without God, and Jesus would not have been promoted without humility. These are the same stipulations that we share with the Messiah. Only God can exalt us, and it is only through humility that we are "eligible" for His upgrade. When we rely on any other source, especially people, to be the cause for our purpose to succeed, we will always come up short.

To establish truth in this matter, here are a couple of things that I have had to learn through personal error, and through seeing others slip deeply into the vortex of these traps.

1. Do not believe it is someone else's fault. Humans have the tendency to blame others for not being in the position they believe they deserve. You are not being held back because so-and-so did not pick you, endorse your name, or give you a chance to "shine" in your spiritual giftings. The blooming of our purpose is not anyone's but God's responsibility. Absolutely no one can hold us back or keep us down, because when God wants to launch us to a new level, no one can interfere with that but us.

> "I know that You can do all things, and that no purpose of Yours can be thwarted."
> (Job 42:2 NASB)

2. Let go of any entitlement attitude. I can honestly say we have derailed from the basic principles of our faith once we begin to treat God like someone who owes us something. God is not in debt to us. Any blessing, favor, breakthrough, promotion, and spiritual gift is given to us by the grace of God. I understand that faith tells us we should all be living in expectation and I am well aware of every Biblical concept such as sowing and reaping. But I also know that we should be doing things for God—not so we can receive a reward, but because we are His humble servants responding in love.

It is disheartening when we create a credence towards the role of God that says, "I did this, so now you have to do that." When we are only interested in completing a "transaction," doing just to get something, then our entire interaction with God can be very cold and non-relational.

Entitlement is the belief that we inherently have the right to a certain kind of special treatment and recognition. If God or someone else doesn't give us what we feel we deserve, then they are in the wrong and we are the "victims."

After the resurrection of Christ, the apostles of the New Testament never once exclaimed with a sense of entitlement that God owes them for all their sacrifice, service, and endurance during persecution. It was just the opposite. They lived as though they were the ones that "owed" God. Serving Jesus in every season—whether good or bad—was a wonderful honor, pure delight, and the least the apostles felt they could do. In Luke 17, Jesus addresses entitlement and reminds us that we are not the "boss." We are privileged to serve the real "boss," God—and be a part of bringing Heaven to Earth. Verse 10 (TPT) declares: "we are just doing what is expected of us and fulfilling our duties." This lesson of Jesus was not meant to provoke a works-and-performance mentality, but was used to present the right perspective and reverence.

If anything, Jesus was the only person who was entitled. He was God's beloved Son who had done no wrong and did not deserve to be crucified for our sins. Instead of demanding "His rights," Jesus willingly laid down His entitlement.

> "Though he was God, he did not think of equality with God as something to cling to. Instead, he gave up his divine privileges; he took the humble position of a slave and was born as a human being. When he appeared in human form, he humbled himself in obedience to God and died a criminal's death on a cross."
> (Philippians 2:6-8 NLT)

One of the grandest gestures of humility we can render is to give up our rights and be willing to surrender what we think we deserve so that others can experience Jesus. Paul said it like this: "Now, even though I am free from obligations to others, I joyfully make myself a servant to all in order to win as many converts as possible" (1 Corinthians 9:19 TPT). When we are truly serving the Lord without any ulterior motives, there will be no strings attached. Any other reason for serving will breed a spirit of entitlement and eventually a prideful heart. As long as blame and entitlement exist in our venture with God, delay is inevitable.

IN THE WAITING

Season of Humility

One of my pastors, Keith-Alan, went through what we playfully call "a season of humility." Nearly eight years ago, Keith-Alan was serving and leading as the main Sunday preacher to the Junior High schoolers at a thriving, mega-size church. At the same time, he was serving our specialty ministry on Sunday evenings and leading some of our outreaches, such as our rap-battles and live shows. Keith-Alan was the host and "face" of these events and began to really excel in this area of ministry. He has a God-given ability to lead and capture people's attention and that gift was beginning to show and shine.

Then came the dilemma. Aury and I were separating from the mega-church to pioneer Life150 Church, and Keith-Alan was torn. He needed to decide if he would stay and continue to grow in his promising position as a youth leader or walk away and join us. Through a time of prayer and fasting, the Lord had drawn him to team up with us and help build our starter church.

Prior to this moment, Keith-Alan has had quite a few encounters with prophetic leaders in the body of Christ that have revealed to him that he would be a pastoral voice for this young generation. Therefore, by sacrificing his role with the youth at the mega-church, he assumed a greater opportunity would automatically be waiting for him. With a prophetic calling declared over his life, competent ministry experience, and a natural demeanor for leadership, it only made sense for him to not have to start from scratch but instead be brought into an openly, influential position. That was not the case whatsoever. Remember, God does things through process and Keith-Alan was definitely about to experience it.

With only a few weeks before launching the church in a hotel ballroom, I had to round up the troops and begin to divide the responsibilities of the "house" with those who desired to serve in our community. In that process, I did not ask Keith-Alan to lead any of our teams. Instead he was called to be a part of the crew that sets up and breaks down the sound equipment and other general stations of the church. It was a position that operated behind the scenes, requiring the team to arrive hours before anyone else did and stay after everyone had gone home. It was not my intention to keep Keith-Alan out of the "limelight" of ministry. I knew his leadership potential from years of working side-by-side with him. But for some reason, even when it was time to recruit someone to lead the crew, I chose someone that had only been with the church for a few months.

For several years, Keith-Alan gave his best for the Lord while serving in the background, concealing his sacrificial labor from the public eye. In that time, not once did he give Aury and I the impression that he was dissatisfied because we did not recognize his "star" quality anointing like the other church did. There were no off-beat, self-promoting hints insinuating we "owed" him and were obligated to advance his calling for all that he has given to the church. I never once felt pressured, even when we ordained many leaders, elders, and pastors before him. Because it was not up to me, but God, to move him forward. When you truly, wholeheartedly commit your service to Jesus, you will never expect man to be the one who promotes you. There is no blame and entitlement, just pure trust in the Lord, the only one who has the power to exalt you.

To bring this story to a close, the reason we called this his "season of humility" was because anytime we needed him to help in an area that would draw attention to his service, something unusually embarrassing would happen. For instance, Keith-Alan wanted to help us run the sound during the service when we were shorthanded. Strangely enough, every time he would step behind the sound booth a distracting, loud feedback would blare out of the speakers, causing the people to glance at the sound booth thinking, "what is this guy doing?" One time, he left the sound area to visit the bathroom while I was in the middle of preaching and my microphone battery died. The entire congregation just waited until Keith-Alan completed his business and when he returned, he was met with a room full of people giggling over another awkward scenario.

My favorite moment that we still laugh about to this day was when I needed to move a heavy audio speaker to the other side of the room. Like an action hero, Keith-Alan darted over to "rescue" his pastor from a weighty task, confidently exclaiming before the morning crew, "Put that down pastor, I got this, this is what I do." Pleased with his gesture of letting me know he's got my back, he lifted the heavy item and took a few steps, only to fumble in his footing and land directly on his face. Everyone rushed over to ask if he was okay—and with his face-cheek mashed against the floor and buttocks landscaped towards the sky, he sheepishly answered, "This is a season of humility."

There were many more amusing incidents that would follow, but despite these episodes Keith-Alan would continue to faithfully serve and honor any position he was given, embracing the waiting, until the Lord God alone would exalt him.

> "The one who manages the little he has been given with faithfulness and integrity will be promoted and trusted with greater responsibilities. But those who cheat with the little they have been given will not be considered trustworthy to receive more."
> (Luke 16:10 TPT)

Patience is Surrender

The waiting is the humblest place to be in the life of a Jesus follower. It takes humility to surrender to a process that is intentionally there to test our strength and character, confront the depths of our heart and the purity of our motives, and transform every bit of our identity and nature. To put it plainly, patience is the perfect picture of surrender, and surrender is the greatest acknowledgment of our love and commitment to Christ.

The promise is reserved for the humble and humility is exclusively established in the waiting. We need the waiting. I pray that you will begin to perceive this as the most treasured time in your life. For it is only in the waiting that you are becoming, and what you become in the waiting is who you will be in the promise.

> "So don't be impatient for the Lord to act; keep moving forward steadily in his ways, and he will EXALT YOU AT THE RIGHT TIME. And when he does, you will possess every promise, including your full inheritance..."
>
> (Psalm 37:34 TPT, emphasis added)

11

Faith for the Promises

The promises of God are not guaranteed. Just because He promised you something, it does not mean it will come to pass. I know upon hearing this, many might doctrinally challenge such a statement, claiming, "God does not lie" (see Numbers 23:19 NLT). It is true that God does not and cannot lie, but the promise needs our participation for it to be brought to completion.

God made many promises in the Bible that were not fulfilled. Here is a covenant God professed over the first generation of Israelites that broke out of Egypt.

> "I have promised to rescue you from your oppression in Egypt. I will lead you to a land flowing with milk and honey..."
> (Exodus 3:17 NLT)

The Israelites had the God of the universe backing them up and He committed to a pledge of granting these former slaves a prosperous place to call home. Sadly, they did not experience this bountiful land of promise. The agreement that God had made was annulled, due to the fact that they never changed into the people He was training them to be. Although God had given His word, He was not bound to award an assembly who constantly embraced the idols of their enemies and were unfaithful to the things of God.

A father may sincerely promise his daughter a new vehicle for her sixteenth birthday, but is he still obligated if his daughter is coming home intoxicated, failing in her classes at school, and responding disobediently to her mother? Absolutely not! No one in their right mind would accuse the father of being unfair for withholding the promised car from his daughter, because it was not his lack of integrity that canceled the deal but her lack of maturity and readiness. In fact, if the father did decide to overlook his daughter's reckless behavior and go ahead and gift his daughter with a new ride, we would deem the father irresponsible.

God does make promises over our lives. But above that, He is a loving, responsible Father. He regards our preparation for the promise more important than the promise itself. If the Israelites would have trusted the Lord to lead them instead of being quick to blame Him for every hold up and hindrance that took place during the wilderness experience, they would have become the greatest nation on Earth. Let's make sure we do not make the same mistake and miss it like they did. We must be clear on the fact that God is never the one setting us back. We are the only ones that can work with or work against the promises and prophecies that are proclaimed over our lives.

Where do I Begin?

We move towards the calling and destiny on our life by the seeds we sow, the foundation we build, the humility of our character, our mature motives, and everything else that develops in the waiting.

Sometimes viewing a "list" of Christian characteristics that must evolve can overwhelm us, but it is truly meant to equip us for the great things ahead. The anxiousness of "becoming" subsides when we realize it is not about frantically striving to be a "better" Christian, but more about relationship. Every one of these qualities of Christ that is in us has the ability to naturally progress when our main pursuit is an intimate connection with the Lord.

The husband I became for my wife radiated from my love for her. As I cultivated my care and godly thoughts towards her, Christ-like traits of a husband ripened on its own. I did not need to "try" and be a servant or supportive; these were things that naturally developed while simply enjoying my relationship with the love of my life.

Enjoying our relationship with Jesus is where it all begins. If that is missing, it will be a feeble effort to find the person God designed you to be. Colossians 2:10 NASB says: "And in Him you have been made complete…" which means the more of Him that you have, the more of you that you'll see.

If you have never asked Jesus to be your Savior and opened yourself up to a loving relationship with a faithful God, you can do this now. Take a serious moment to accept complete forgiveness of your sins through the sacrifice of Jesus, the gracious gift of eternal salvation, and internal peace and freedom from the finished work of the cross. If you are making this decision for the first time, a great next move would be to find a church community that will help you grow, understand the Word of God, and nurture your new relationship with the Lord.

Breathing Life

Prayerfully by now this book has broadened your insight on the necessity of the process, helped you to understand what takes place during that time, and revealed what is your integral part in it all. Once you feel you have initiated these revelations, you must learn to sustain them. Every breakthrough and divine promotion that are within the promises of God, must have life-giving power infused in them to combat everything that would attempt to resist its fulfillment. This leads me to the mission of this final chapter—to breathe life into your promises.

Romans 4:16 TPT says: "The promise depends on faith." As believers with a diabolical entity that does not want us to succeed, we have to ignite a steadfast lifestyle of faith. It is imperative that we do not let the truth of our destiny be drowned out from the voice of the enemy, whose aim is to get us to believe that the waiting is a waste. We can never let the enemy's assault against our identity and future have more "volume" than the truth and promises of God. That is why we need faith as our megaphone to amplify truth when truth is hidden from us.

Let's now examine the activation of faith that we need for promises by the power of our words.

> "Your words are so powerful that they will KILL or give LIFE…"
> (Proverbs 18:21 TPT, emphasis added)

We are always sowing seeds when we speak. Our words are either adding life or breeding death to the future God has for us. Have you listened to your words lately? What are they creating while you're in the waiting?

In the third chapter of the book of James, he metaphorically compares the confession of our words to a tiny rudder that has the strength to direct the path of a massive ship sailing through rough waters. That sure is a lot of power for such a small object—and so are the declarations we speak by faith or by fear. In fact, our constant confessions can literally steer the course of our lives.

Jesus said that every word that He speaks are Spirit and life (see John 6:63 TPT). We need to be in that same place of speaking life by the Holy Spirit and forming the will of God for our lives.

You honestly cannot afford to withhold life-giving decrees, especially when you have a hateful enemy, challenging circumstances, and past failures that are determined to bring death to your destiny. Failing to speak life to counter these attacks with the Word of God can almost be like agreeing with these "death threats."

Energy

Hebrews 4:12 TPT says: "For we have the living Word of God, which is full of energy..." We know that the Word of God is alive, but what does the passage mean by calling it energy? In the Aramaic, energy can be rendered as "all effective." But the translation that stands out to me the most is the word "energes" derived from the Greek lexicon. It defines the word as a never ending, active, supernatural force. The law of physics proves that all things are in a constant state of motion. Everything on Earth moves and vibrates, even the tiniest, subatomic particle is electrically charged with life. Now imagine the sonic surge injected in the Word of the Almighty; the one who called and created everything into existence by His words (see Genesis 1 NKJV). As His ambassadors with the official seal of Heavenly authority, we have permission to advance and "energize" His purposes and promises by His divine Word.

Are you ready to begin declaring the Word of God? I know some of us might be afraid. We fear disappointment. We think, "what if I declare the Word of God, wait, and nothing happens?" Here is my advice for that—do not stop until something happens.

Jesus painted a parabolic picture in Luke chapter 18 to inspire the apostles to never stop praying and never lose hope. The story brings us into the scenario of a poor widow who brought her case to a callous, civil rights judge who deliberately kept ignoring her urgent request for justice. Eventually, after a certain amount of time, the stubborn judge ruled in the widow's favor, claiming that it was her persistent asking that made him grant her appeal. The narrative ends with Jesus summarizing His point on persistence, making it clear that those who cry out night and day, without backing down, will also receive their request.

In this next passage, Jesus emphasizes this thought again. This time without any analogy or allegory but instead laying it before us in plain sight.

> "So I say to you, ask and keep on asking, and it will be given to you; seek and keep on seeking, and you will find; knock and keep on knocking, and the door will be opened to you. For everyone who keeps on asking [persistently], receives; and he who keeps on seeking [persistently], finds; and to him who keeps on knocking [persistently], the door will be opened."
>
> (Luke 11:9-10 AMP)

Faith and Patience

To keep on asking, keep on seeking, and keep on knocking seems simple enough—or maybe not. This is what challenges many believers, because it requires two things that we normally lack the ability to do at the same time. You can see them expressed through the writing of James: "brothers and sisters, we must be PATIENT and filled with EXPECTATION…" (see James 5:7 TPT, emphasis added). Does God actually insist we live in absolute expectation (faith) in every situation and walk in complete patience, awaiting the outcome with a good attitude no matter how long it takes? It is certainly possible, but we usually get stuck here because to fully expect and fully be patient is a combo that is foreign to us.

Here is where the trouble begins. If we know God is asking us to be patient, we have the tendency to lower our expectation, because waiting without knowing is scary. We figure, expecting less will protect us from being let down. The truth is, if we expect less we receive less. The other side of the coin is: if God is asking us to dig in and radically expect the impossible, we might think that this has to happen quickly, because there is no way I can be patient if I am firing faith on all cylinders. How can I be patient and content if every day I am putting all my energy in believing?

These twisted theories have held us back and robbed us from taking Bible-size risks. If anything, history reveals the only way the patriarchs received the full reward of their calling was through the union of faith and patience. We need both if we want the promises of God.

> "So don't allow your hearts to grow dull or sluggish but follow the example of those who fully received what God has promised because of their strong FAITH and PATIENT endurance."
> (Hebrews 6:12 TPT, emphases added)

Getting faith is one thing, but keeping faith is an entirely different issue. Let me put it this way: You can get faith through a strong encounter with the truth, but you can only *keep* faith if you are a person who knows how to patiently endure. Faith will always slip out of our hands without patience.

I was recently listening to a message online from one of my favorite teachers. He shared an extraordinary testimony of a ministry friend of his who had a prophecy from twenty-seven years ago come to pass in a big way. The prophetic word was irrelevant at the time of reception and the man did not know it would take about two-and-a-half decades for it to make sense. All these years he stood in patient expectation, which paid off. Without going into all the details, this minister of the gospel received one-hundred forty acres of land that is worth twenty-four million dollars without paying a penny. Though this gift is a great resource for the next divine project within his calling, he did not sit around and wait for this particular promise to manifest. He occupied during those twenty-seven years by pioneering great moves of God, published books to equip the body of Christ, and raised up thousands of disciples to release the glory of God on the Earth.

My heart for you is to live by the spiritual fruit of patience, enjoying what God is forming within you, without abandoning a passionate pursuit of the promises; to have a risk-filled, unrelenting faith until you see what you're saying with your words.

Releasing Decrees of Faith

I devoted the rest of this chapter to provide a reference as you journey the many moments of process to promise. These are prophetic decrees that have the power to authorize a path that leads to God's plan for us. This does not alleviate the responsibilities of the Biblical principles in this book that we must abide to in order to reach spiritual maturity. These are not magic words that help us to skip the process of humility and a heart transformation. It is an opportunity for you to fasten your faith with the will of God, grow in character, and maximize your effectiveness in the waiting. In Job 22:28 NKJV it says: "...decree a thing, and it will be established for you..." Psalm 2:7 NKJV says: "I will declare the decree the Lord has said to me..." Are you ready to arise and decree the very thing you are becoming and His promises? There is no better time than today to get started.

I have given you seven decrees from each chapter. Every confession is either related to a scripture or a Biblical point written in that chapter. You can boldly profess all of them in one day or do one set per day for ten days. It is up to you. You can even do this every day for a year to empower your steps. You might end up memorizing a few of the decrees that speak to you the most and declare them for the rest of your days. Eventually, you'll want to create your own Biblical decrees to bring life to areas that need the "energes" of God for breakthrough. Whatever you are led to do, do it with all of your heart—knowing that your Heavenly Father loves you tremendously, and He desires that you experience every aspect of the life He designed for you to live, even more than you desire it.

Decrees from Chapter 1
I'm Becoming

1. In the waiting, God is perfecting every part of my being so that nothing is missing or lacking.

2. I am spiritually abounding in maturity as God moves me from one level of glory to another.

3. I do not need to be in control because my trust is in the Lord.

4. Every single spiritual seed I have sown towards my future will become a fruitful harvest.

5. My "food" is to do the will of God and bring it to completion.

6. I will not be troubled by my trials, but rather joyful and confident, knowing that these pressures are developing in me patience, character, and hope.

7. In the waiting, I'm becoming!

Decrees from Chapter 2
Worth the Wait

1. My expectations do not come with deadlines. I will wait patiently for the Lord.

2. Against all odds, when it looks hopeless, I will stand strong. For God is faithful to complete what He has promised.

3. I can do nothing on my own. Today I surrender complete control over to the Father.

4. God is patient with me and I am patient with Him. His plan and purpose is always worth the wait.

5. I will live my life according to the worth of God's amazing grace, for it has made me who I am.

6. I see my short-lived troubles in the light of eternity. I will not focus my attention on what is seen, but on the realm that is unseen.

7. I have a burning passion and love for the living God that radically enforces the fruit of patience in my life.

Decrees from Chapter 3
Save Me from Boredom

1. I am consciously aware and fully occupied with the Kingdom life. I will not make any room for distractions or destructive behaviors.

2. There is absolutely nothing boring about my life. It is thrilling to be an ambassador for the Kingdom of God.

3. Like Nehemiah, I am doing a great work and I cannot come down.

4. I will not make excuses. I have everything I need to be productive and fruitful today.

5. I am faithful over small matters, valuing the very things God has given into my hands. Therefore, I will be trustworthy to rule over greater things.

6. I have taken full advantage of my Heavenly citizenship and Heaven's resources. I will impact and influence my generation for the glory of God.

7. I will not be bored, aimless, or spiritually stagnant. I refuse to just sit and watch life pass me by. I will be active, engaged, and occupied by my wonderful Father's business.

Decrees from Chapter 4
Weary in the Waiting

1. I strengthen myself in the Lord. I will not be overwhelmed, restless, or weary.

2. I will not give up my birthright—my invaluable spiritual inheritance.

3. The things that are sacred in my life will not become common.

4. I will not lose heart while doing good and I will reap everything the Lord has for me.

5. I walk under the influence and power of the Holy Spirit and will not be controlled by the cravings and dominance of the flesh.

6. God's grace is sufficient to make me strong when I am weak.

7. God's Spirit, that never gets weary, dwells inside me. I have an endless supply of strength and power.

Decrees from Chapter 5
Face Forward

1. I have a vision for my future that is beyond my current circumstance.

2. In the waiting, the Lord is preparing me to give birth to a God-ordained vision.

3. I run with passion toward God's direction so that I may reach the purpose that Jesus Christ has called me to fulfill and wants me to discover.

4. I face forward by not dwelling on the negative experiences of the past and fasten my heart to the future.

5. I am not looking backward. I do not have second thoughts. I am future-minded, focused, and moving forward.

6. I have hope-filled thoughts towards my destiny.

7. I am becoming today what I need to be for my future.

Decrees from Chapter 6
The Making of a Masterpiece

1. God has taken the blight, broken, disfigured pieces of my former life and created a beautifully divine masterpiece.

2. I am a chosen vessel for God and my life masterfully shines.

3. Jesus is the author and finisher, founder and perfecter of my life.

4. I am a disciple, embodying the complete nature of my teacher and Rabbi, Jesus.

5. My life makes Jesus visible to the world.

6. If you've seen me, you've seen Jesus.

7. It takes time to create a masterpiece. My life is not forgotten in the waiting, it is formed.

Decrees from Chapter 7
A Storm-Proof Foundation

1. I am not immune to having problems, I have an advantage over them—His name is the Holy Spirit!!!

2. With Jesus, I am thoroughly equipped and empowered to overcome every trial, every temptation, and every test.

3. Quitting is not an option. I may stumble, but I will rise over and over again.

4. I have built my life on stormproof, firm foundations. Nothing can take me down.

5. God has purified my motives. I will not lose my reward.

6. I trust in the Lord with all my heart and I do not lean on my own understanding.

7. As a lover of God, my life is deeply rooted and firmly planted in Him.

Decrees from Chapter 8
Times of Testing

1. Patience is a gift, where my Christ character is formed.

2. As my character is cultivated, my calling is accelerated.

3. Each test I face and pass is drawing me closer to my destiny.

4. In the same way that gold and silver are refined by fire, the Lord purifies my heart by the tests and trials of life.

5. I am tested so I can readily respond to anything that might occur in the path to the promises.

6. My convictions are strong in times of trouble and persecution.

7. My supreme passion is to please God. I will not be drawn away by ungodly desires.

Decrees from Chapter 9
Finding Freedom

1. He who lives in me is greater than he who is in the world.

2. God is able to do exceedingly, abundantly, above all that I can ask or think, according to the power that works in me.

3. I am a new creation and I can do all things through the explosive strength and power of Christ that is infused in me.

4. I was made to be free! I refuse to be restrained and oppressed under the influence of burdens, bitterness, and bondages.

5. I have stripped off every weight that slows me down, so I can run with endurance the race God has set before me.

6. In Christ Jesus, I have rest for my soul.

7. I forgive everyone I have found fault with the same way I have been graciously forgiven by Jesus Christ.

Decrees from Chapter 10
Only God Can

1. The favor that brings promotion and power comes from God. No one can exalt me but Him.

2. I am blessed by trusting in the Lord and making Him my hope and confidence.

3. As I wait upon the Lord, I will birth spiritual Isaacs and not Ishmaels.

4. Because I have humbled myself in the presence of the Lord and left the timing in His hands, He will exalt me.

5. I am free from blaming others and let go of any entitlement attitude. I have taken full responsibility for my spiritual maturity and future.

6. I know that God can do all things, and that no purpose of His can be stopped.

7. I will not be impatient for the Lord to act. I will keep moving forward steadily in His ways. He will exalt me at the right time, and I will possess every promise, including my full inheritance.

Additional Scriptures to Stand on

"...Don't give up; don't be impatient; be entwined as one with the Lord. Be brave and courageous, and never lose hope. Yes, keep on waiting—for he will never disappoint you!"
(Psalm 27:14 TPT)

"What delight comes to you when you wait upon the Lord! For you will find what you long for."
(Matthew 5:4 TPT)

"Patient endurance is what you need now, so that you will continue to do God's will. Then you will receive all that he has promised."
(Hebrews 10:36 NLT)

"The best way to live is with revelation-knowledge, for without it, you'll grow impatient and run right into error."
(Proverbs 19:2 TPT)

"Yet those who wait for the Lord will gain new strength; they will mount up with wings like eagles, they will run and not get tired, they will walk and not become weary."
(Isaiah 40:31 NASB)

"Rest in the Lord and wait patiently for Him; Do not fret because of him who prospers in his way, Because of the man who carries out wicked schemes."
(Psalms 37:7 NASB)

"I waited and waited and waited some more, patiently, knowing God would come through for me. Then, at last, he bent down and listened to my cry. He stooped down to lift me out of danger from the desolate pit I was in, out of the muddy mess I had fallen into. Now he's lifted me up into a firm, secure place and steadied me while I walk along his ascending path."
(Psalms 40:1-2 TPT)

"The Lord is good to those who wait for Him, to the person who seeks Him."
(Lamentations 3:25 NASB)

"…he has given you magnificent promises that are beyond all price, so that through the power of these tremendous promises you can experience partnership with the divine nature…"
(2 Peter 1:4 TPT)

"My life, my every moment, my destiny—it's all in your hands…"
(Psalms 31:15 TPT)

ENDNOTES

Online Article: What really drives you crazy about waiting in line (it actually isn't the wait at all) by Ana Swanson
https://www.washingtonpost.com/news/wonk/wp/2015/11/27/what-you-hate-about-waiting-in-line-isnt-the-wait-at-all/?utm_term=.b9fb1bec555a

Online Article: Are You Part Of The $62 Billion Loss Due To Poor Customer Service? contributor Shep Hyken
https://www.forbes.com/sites/shephyken/2017/04/01/are-you-part-of-the-62-billion-loss-due-to-poor-customer-service/#143d9d557e5f

ABOUT THE AUTHOR

In the late 90's, after working professionally in the dance industry with artists such as Madonna, Will Smith, The Backstreet Boys, and Missy Elliot, Tymme, and his wife, Aury, surrendered their lives to Jesus (testimony is shared in Tymme's first book, *Living Souled Out*). Their passion for God's kingdom and revival in the arts led them to launch Word In Motion Dance Co. and several ongoing events including: Word In Motion's Urban Dance Festival and Step Of Hope Benefit Concert. Tymme and Aury Reitz are now the lead pastors of Life150 Church in N. Hollywood, California, where they provide an opportunity for all to experience and express the unfailing love and power of Jesus. From the unique worship that occasionally fuses contemporary with rap, to the prophetic dancers, to the message and loving community, Life150 Church gatherings are designed to radically encounter the Kingdom of God in a real way.

Please visit my website www.tymmereitz.com